Oı

In a Million

A mile-by-mile guide to Southwest

Colorado's Million Dollar

Highway and the San Juan Skyway

Branson Reynolds

One Drive in a Million

A mile-by-mile guide to Southwest Colorado's Million Dollar Highway and the San Juan Skyway

Branson Reynolds

ISBN-13: 978-1-4566-2731-7

Book Design by Branson Reynolds

Published eBookIt.com

One Drive in a Million
A mile-by-mile guide to Southwest Colorado's Million Dollar Highway and the San Juan Skyway

Branson Reynolds

CONTENTS

Introduction 1

Using this Guide 3

Road Designations 4

The Drive..5

    Durango to Silverton 6

    Silverton to Ouray 37

    Ouray to Ridgeway..54

    Ridgway to Placerville...................................57

    Placerville to Telluride 63

    Telluride to Rico and Dolores............................69

    Dolores to Cortez--Official Route 93

    Cortez towards Mancos and Durango 98

    U.S Hwy #160: Mancos to Durango 101

Appendix..111

    Altitude Sickness 111

    Clothing Suggestions 111

    Camping 112

    National Forest Campgrounds 113

    Useful Telephone #'s 114

The San Juan Skyway

Introduction

Scenic view of San Juans

One of the most spectacular drives in North America, the San Juan Skyway is a 236 mile loop which winds through forests of aspen and pine, over high passes with stunning panoramic views of mountain ranges exceeding 14,000 feet in elevation, through historic mining towns which played important roles in the colorful history of Southwest Colorado, and past the World Heritage Site of Mesa Verde.

In 1988 this drive was designated as one of 54 National Scenic Byways, and was later chosen #1 of 10 to be designated as All American Roads for their natural beauty and historical significance. Along the way you may see black bear or mountain lions crossing the highway or elk and deer grazing in the meadows. A portion of this route includes the famous Million Dollar Highway which negotiates the awesome Uncompahgre Gorge, high in the Rocky Mountains between Silverton and Ouray, Colorado.

To the first Spanish explorers who visited this area, possibly as early as Coronado's expedition in 1540, they were known as the "Sierra Madres", the "Mother Mountains". Today the magnificent ranges of the La Platas, the Needles, the San Miguels, the Wilsons, and the Grenadiers, all merge before you into the heart of the San Juan Mountains. The majesty and beauty of these mountains is so great that they were originally proposed as the site for Rocky Mountain National Park, later located north of Denver. The number of private land holdings in the form of old mining claims prevented national park status, but the awesome beauty remains.

With time, the deserted towns and mines have become a part of the landscape. Animas Forks, Guston, Red Mountain City, Alta, the North Star, Silver Ledge and the Yankee Girl sit abandoned but full of nostalgia as they decay amidst some of the most stunning mountain scenery in North America.

Use this book as a guide to the natural and cultural history of the San Juans, and as a point-by-point reference to interesting sites and places of inspiring natural beauty that you will encounter along the Skyway. Also noted are National Forest campgrounds, intersecting roads, hiking trails, visitor's centers, National Forest Service offices, and other useful information.

Travel the Skyway and experience what is truly "One Drive in a Million!

2

Using this Guide

As you travel the Skyway, mile-markers will serve as reference points. These markers are placed every mile between major highway junctions, the numbers getting larger going in one direction, and smaller going the other. The mileages are seen as white numbers against a green background located on metal posts along the highway.

The bold numbers in the guide represent the mile markers along the route. Locations in the guide are recorded to the nearest tenth of a mile beyond the last marker. Different odometers often give slightly different measurements and markers are also sometimes missing due to removal by snowplows, etc., so consider the mileages given between markers as close approximations.

Road Designations

The following road designations are used in the guide. They correspond with designations given on maps of the San Juan and Uncompahgre National Forests through which you will be traveling. Use your own judgment when traveling off of the Skyway, but remember it's easy to follow a road for a ways, and then discover you can't go forward and you can't turn around.

4WD-should not be attempted except in four-wheel drive, high-clearance vehicles.

Primitive-may be negotiable without 4WD or high-clearance vehicles, but not recommended.

Improved-graded dirt or gravel roads are generally suitable for all vehicles in dry weather. Watch out if it's wet!

F.R. - Forest Road

N.F.S. - National Forest Service

C.R. - County Road

The Drive

Durango from Smelter Mountain

Following the Skyway
Durango to Silverton

Downtown Durango

You can begin using this guide from any point along the Skyway and follow it in either direction, but here we will begin by heading north from downtown Durango on Main Street (U.S. Hwy. #550) towards mile-marker #25, which is located a little over a mile north of North 32nd Street on the east side of the highway. We'll follow the Skyway in a counter-clockwise direction through Silverton, Ouray, Ridgway, Telluride, Dolores, Cortez, Mancos, and back to our starting point in Durango. If traveling in a clockwise direction, the tenths-of-a-mile distances will not work but it is still relatively easy to locate the locations mentioned between the markers.

While other adventurers and fortune hunters were here earlier, the first verified visit by white men to the pleasant valley at the bend in the river where Durango now stands was in 1765 when Spaniards, under the leadership of 86 yr. old Juan Rivera, left Santa Fe and headed north to the San Juan River. From here they followed the Animas River north into the San Juans in search of gold and silver.

In July, 1776, another expedition led by Franciscan friars Francisco Antanasizo Dominguez and Silvestre Velez de Escalante left Santa Fe following the same route as Rivera. They then headed west in search of a route from Santa Fe to the Spanish missions in California. Although they found the rugged Colorado Plateau country impassable, forcing their return to Santa Fe, their effort is considered one of the most adventurous explorations of the West ever undertaken.

In the following years, more explorations were made by trappers, prospectors, and adventurers. White settlement began in 1874 when a town site was laid out a few miles west of present-day Durango near the La Plata River. By 1880 the population of Parrot City, named after a San Francisco banker who had financially backed the prospectors, had reached 300.

Just four years after the settlement of Parrot City, another community, Animas City, was founded on the banks of the Animas River within the northern boundaries of present-day Durango. A few of the old rock buildings from these early days may still be seen in the area of North Main Avenue and 32nd Street. One of the oldest buildings still standing is the stone house just south of North City Market.

By the late 1870's the Denver & Rio Grande Railroad had begun laying tracks westward from Denver towards the rich mining region of the San Juan Mountains. Other standard gauge railroads were competing for the riches of the San Juans, but the narrow-gauge lines of the Denver & Rio Grande, with their three-foot wide tracks, beat the competition whose four-foot-eight-inch wide tracks took more time to lay and were more difficult to negotiate on the sharp mountain curves.

The original plan was for the tracks to reach Animas City, but disputes with the city resulted in the railroad building its own town just to the south. When the tracks reached here in August 1881, a tent-city of 3,000 was waiting. Named after another Durango located in Mexico, the new town soon became the largest and most important city in the region.

Durango was a wild place in those days. Quoting from the Solid Muldoon, one of Durango's early newspapers, first published in 1891: "When the sun has tired of shining on the busy hive of Durango, and the moon peeps over some mighty hilltop, the hour is nigh in which our nightly carnival takes place." And, "There is probably not a man in Durango who does not carry on his person a double action six-shooting revolver." For a sense of Durango's early days, visit the La Plata County Historical Society Museum located at 3065 West 2nd Street. For information call 970-259-2402.

Originating in the mountains high above Silverton, the churning waters of the Animas River are hidden in the depths of the rugged Animas

Gorge before emerging into the Animas Valley north of Durango. From here it joins the San Juan River near Aztec, New Mexico, and together their waters flow west, joining the Colorado River at Lake Powell, then southward through Lake Mead and on towards the Sea of Cortez.

Running through Durango, the "Rio de las Animas Perdidos en Purgatorio", the "River of Lost Souls in Purgatory ", was named after Spanish soldiers died in a battle with Ute Indians near here and, lacking a priest to perform the last rights, were doomed to remain forever in Purgatory. Known today simply as the Animas River, it was one of the last free-flowing rivers in the country until the completion of the Animas-La Plata project in 2015 which was built to settle Indian water rights claims with local tribes.

Overuse of water along with years of serious drought had caused siltation at the mouth of the Colorado, blocking what water was left from reaching the sea. The "Minute 319" pulse flow project was an effort to reconnect the river to the sea. And for the first time in years, on May 15, 2014, the Mighty Colorado was once again united with the sea.

The size and shape of the Animas Valley is the result of the scouring action of glaciers during the last 80,000 years. About 11,000 years ago, these glaciers began their last retreat with a warming of the climate that peaked about 5,000 years ago. For millennia, the valley has been an important winter feeding area for elk which still gather here in large numbers in the winter.

The valley was an important hunting ground for the Ute Indians, and it earlier was home to the ancient Puebloan people, the famous "Cliff Dwellers of the Mesa Verde." Ester's Cave, where the naturally mummified remains of the most famous of the Cliff Dwellers was found, is hidden in the red cliffs to the west. Ester now resides in the museum at Mesa Verde National Park.

25.0
Along here are good views of the Animas River.

Animas River

25.6
C.R. #203, which follows the west side of the valley as far as Hermosa before intersecting Hwy. #550, was the main road through the valley before the modern highway was built.

From here the massive West Needle Mountains dominate the view beyond the northern end of the Animas Valley. An early ranch in this area was known as "Waterfall Ranch" after a small waterfalls west of the highway which cascades down the cliff when water is plentiful. A hiking trail leaves C.R. #203 near the base of the falls and leads into Hidden Valley, a public-use area known for its natural beauty and as a wintering ground for elk.

30.0

East of the highway is a housing development known as Dalton Ranch, named for the family that originally owned the land. Two family members, Emit and Grat, were leaders of the infamous "Dalton Gang", known for daring bank robberies throughout the southwest.

30.3

A short distance west on the old stage road known as Trimble Lane (C.R. #252) is Trimble Hot Springs, whose hot sulfur waters were used for centuries by Indians, then by white settlers of the valley. The popularity of the springs grew until the facilities included the beautiful Hermosa House, with its riding stables, saloon and dance hall. Many famous people including Clark Gable and Marilyn Monroe have delighted in these waters. Although fire has destroyed the facilities three times, today you can enjoy a large swimming pool, a hot springs pool, and private hot tubs.

Turn right on Trimble Lane and you will intersect East Animas Road (C.R. #250), on the east side of the valley. Turn left when you reach C.R. #250 and you will soon come to F.R. #682, which heads up Missionary Ridge, named by early settlers for its resemblance to a famous Civil War battleground near Chattanooga, Tennessee. This improved road winds for miles into the back country, but for a short, pleasant drive, try Wallace Lake which is two miles beyond the highway.

Returning to C.R. #250, turn right and you will reconnect with Hwy. #550 at m.m. #35.2. If you return to Hwy. #550 the way you came, turn right at the highway and you will soon cross Hermosa

Creek. Just ahead is an old water tower at the site of Hermosa, which in the late 1880's was a stagecoach and railroad stop with a population of 200.

To the west is C.R. #203, which is an access road into 85,000 acres of wild and roadless country along Hermosa Creek. Just over four miles from the junction, it ends at the head of the Hermosa Creek Trail, which is popular for hiking, bicycling and horseback riding. Several trails within a few miles of the trailhead connect the Hermosa Creek Trail to the Highline Trail, which is part of the 486 mile long Colorado Trail, providing non-motorized access to vast areas of wilderness between Durango and Denver. The trail passes through seven national forests, five major river drainages, and crosses the Continental Divide 12 times. Its highest point is 13,271-feet above sea level, and most of the trail is above 10,000 ft. in elevation

33.5
On the far side of the valley you can see C.R. #682 angling up Missionary Ridge.

35.2
There are numerous hot-springs in this area, and one bubbles to the surface beside the highway just ahead. Its waters once served a nearby resort known as Pinkerton Hot Springs, named after Judge Pinkerton who settled here in 1875. These waters were often used by the famous Ute Chief Ouray for their healing powers.

Ahead is C.R. #250 which soon splits, with the left fork heading north to reconnect with Hwy. #550 near m.m. #37. The right fork soon crosses the Animas River on Baker's Bridge, which was named after Charles Baker, an early mountain man and explorer of the San Juans. Beyond the bridge, C.R. #250 loops back and follows along the east side of the Animas Valley back towards Durango.

Until 1876 the only access to Silverton was on foot or horseback. In that year, a toll road from the upper end of the Animas Valley to Silverton was opened with the bridge as its southern terminus. The original Baker's Bridge was used for over 50 years until a flood destroyed it in 1911. Remember the scene from Butch Cassidy and the Sundance Kid were Butch and the Kid jumped from a high cliff into a raging river? These are the cliffs and that is the river.

36.6

Here the Hwy. #550 bridge crosses above the tracks of the Durango & Silverton Narrow Gauge Railroad, providing an excellent vantage point to view and photograph the train. Drive over the bridge and walk back over the bridge to photograph the train as it approaches the overpass. Check the train's departure schedule at the depot in town (888-872-4607) and allow approximately 45 minutes for the train to reach this point.

Durango & Silverton Narrow-Gauge Train

37.3

C.R. #250 rejoins Hwy. #550 here. About half-a-mile from the highway it crosses the railroad tracks, providing another easily accessible location for photographing the train.

37.4

Wildlife is abundant year-round in the Animas Valley, and many elk and deer are killed as they attempt to cross the highway. The high fence along here is an attempt to reduce the numbers of large mammals meeting this fate.

There is a gain in elevation of over 4,000 feet between the Animas Valley and the top of Coal Bank Pass, the first major pass north of Durango. For every thousand feet gain in elevation, you will encounter environmental changes equivalent to driving north several hundred miles, and a drop in average temperature of around 3 degrees F.

You are now in the Transition Zone which lies between 7,000 and 8,500 feet. Here, the Upper Sonoran Life Zone, characteristic of the Durango area, makes the transition from sagebrush and forests of Pinion Pine and Juniper to a more moist zone of Ponderosa Pine, Gamble Oak and Douglas Fir. Shilona Lake, which is on private property and closed to the public, can be seen to the east.

Bull and cow Elk

38.0

You are now in the San Juan National Forest, which encompasses over two million acres of wild country and is home to big game animals such as elk, deer, bighorn sheep, mountain goats, lions, and black bear. It's possible that a few grizzlies still roam the distant wilderness.

The surrounding Weiminuche Wilderness was named for the Ute Indians who once roamed these mountains. Known as the "Blue Sky People" by surrounding tribes, they call themselves "Nuche", which means "The People". This is one of the country's largest wilderness areas, which are lands designated by Congress to be protected and preserved in their natural condition without permanent improvements or habitation.

38.5

C.R. #200 soon ends at Rockwood, where a small settlement had been established by the late 1870's. The railroad reached here in 1881, and Chinese laborers lived here while laying the tracks up the gorge of the Animas River.

39.4

After the railroad reached Rockwood, the stage picked up passengers and followed the Rico Road through the present location of Tamarron Resort, continuing north to the Hermosa Park road near Purgatory, then west over Scotch Creek Pass to Rico. This old road is now a National Historic Landmark. Portions of the film Avalanche starring Rock Hudson and Mia Farrow were filmed here.

For hundreds of millions of years mountain ranges have risen and eroded away again where the San Juans now stand. Ancient seas repeatedly flooded the landscape, depositing layer upon layer of silt. The 2,000 foot Hermosa Formation, seen in the Hermosa Cliffs along the west side of the valley, was formed during this time.

40.7

The Goulding Creek Trail begins on the west side of the highway and climbs quickly to the top of the Hermosa Cliffs. This is a relatively difficult trail but worth the effort as it leads to a scenic, secluded valley and great views in all directions.

41.7

The Chris Park N.F.S Campground is a couple of miles from the highway on CR #671. It has three large sites which are available by reservation (877-444-6777). The Haviland Lake N.F.S. Campground (45 sites) is a ways further on the other side of the lake. Here you'll find good fishing and great views of Engineer Mountain to the northwest and the Needle Mountains to the east. The Animas-Silverton Wagon Road passed through here in 1876 and operated for six years until the opening of the railroad. Southeast of the campground, a 4WD road leads a mile to Forebay Lake for more secluded fishing and camping.

43.8

East of the highway is Electra Lake, whose waters once powered a hydroelectric plant at Tacoma, a railroad company town located on the Animas River three miles above Rockwood. The lake, originally known as Ignacio Reservoir, is closed to the public.

44.0

You are now in the Canadian Life Zone, which lies between 8,500 and 10,000 feet in elevation. Wetter and cooler than the Transition Zone, here you encounter vast forests of aspen, pine and fir. While the evergreens remain green year-round, it's the aspen that mark the seasons in the high country. Their graceful white trunks, supporting plumes of fiery reds, oranges and yellows, make autumn in the Rockies a memorable experience.

Aspens prefer open, sunny slopes and are among the first trees to repopulate areas ravaged by fire. Spreading primarily from new sprouts growing from the existing root system, aspens, until recently, were thought to be the world's largest living organism, with trees growing from the same root system often covering several acres. That honor now belongs to a type of mushroom in Oregon's Blue Mountains whose root system can measure over 2 ½ miles across.

46.3
You are approaching the Needles Store, with the last gas before Silverton. To the east are the jagged spires of Sunlight, Eolus, and Windom. It was these peaks that gave the Needle Mountains their name.

47.0
On the west side of the highway is a large boulder said to have been a favorite hiding place for robbers awaiting the stage between Durango and Silverton.

48.9
C.R. #593 just ahead leads to the Purgatory National Forest Campground. This trail heads down through the dense forest on steep switchbacks to Purgatory Flats on Cascade Creek. This is a popular area for overnight camping or as a rest stop for hikers going on to the Animas River Trail.

49.0
The Purgatory Resort, named after nearby Purgatory Creek, boasts over 35 miles of ski runs ranging from 8,000 to over 10,000 ft. in elevation.

Also offered in the summer are zipline adventures, an alpine slide, and other fun activities. Call 800-525-0892 for information.

Just ahead is another great view of the Needle Mountains. Take advantage of the pull-out for an opportunity to view or photograph the beauty of the San Juans.

Needle Mountains

49.5

The Hermosa Park Road (F.R. #578) leads into the Hermosa Valley, which is Spanish for beautiful. This is an improved road for six miles to the Sig Creek N.F.S. Campground (9 sites). Regular cars are fine to this point but the road soon gets rough and gains elevation quickly as it follows Hermosa Creek past the remains of the old Greysill Mine and through beautiful forests of aspen, spruce, and fir.

The road then splits, with one branch going over Bolam Pass, treating you to spectacular views of the Wilson Mountains and Lizard Head Peak near Telluride. There are good camping locations along the drive and at the top of the pass. The road then descends into the Dolores River Valley, a few miles north of Rico at the Cayton N.F.S. Campground. The other branch follows the old Rico stage road through dense forests along Scotch Creek before intersecting Hwy. #145 a few miles south of Rico.

The first white men known to have entered what is now San Juan County arrived in 1860 when mountaineer Charles Baker led a group of prospectors into the area. No attempt was made to establish a permanent settlement or to mine, though prospecting in the area occurred sporadically for the next several years until rich veins of silver ore were discovered and active mining began in 1873.

A major obstacle to mining was that the area belonged to the Ute Indians. The Burnot Treaty of 1873 quickly solved the problem, giving the Utes $1,000 for the entire 3,000,000 acres of San Juan County, and sending troops to "assist" them in moving to their present location south of Durango. Huge reserves of natural gas were later discovered on their land, making them today one of the richest per capita people in the world.

50.0
The old wooden corral just ahead is a great location for viewing and photographing 12,698 ft. Engineer Mountain, straight ahead, and Grizzly Peak to its left.

Engineer Mountain

50.4

Along here are several beaver dams and lodges. Beavers are the world's second-largest rodent with adults weighing around 40 lbs. The world's largest rodent, the South American Capybara, can reach 150 lbs.

By providing still, deep waters as protection against predators and to float food and building materials, these "busy beavers" have changed the face of the earth more than any animal other than man by damming streams which eventually silt in, leading to the formation of new valleys.

51.0

Just after crossing Cascade Creek, an improved road on the left with beautiful waterfalls, cascades, and primitive camping along the way leads a couple of miles to a popular starting point for hiking and horseback trips further into the mountains. From here a relatively long but lovely hiking trail follows the creek to its headwaters in an alpine cirque. This trail was an early Ute pack trail going up Cascade Creek, around Bear Mountain, and down Mineral Creek into the valley where Silverton now stands.

A short distance beyond Cascade Creek on the east side of the highway is the southern end of the old Lime Creek Road (F.R. #591). This was another Indian trail that went up Lime Creek and down Bear Creek and Mineral Creek into the Silverton Valley. By 1905, the Lime Creek Road was part of the first complete public wagon road between Durango and Silverton. Reconnecting with Hwy. #550 at m.m. #59.6, the road offers a beautiful 12 mile drive suitable for high clearance 4XD vehicles.

Three miles from the highway the road reaches a peaceful pond covered with bright yellow lilies in the summer. A well-marked and easy trail from here leads to Potato Lake on the eastern slope of 11,871 ft. Potato Mountain, commonly known as Spud Mountain. Due to the ease of the hike and beauty of the surroundings, this is a popular hike for families and children. Along the way you may encounter a variety of wildlife such as deer and elk, and it is a popular area for birdwatching.

West Needle Mountains

Beyond here the road narrows and gets rougher with sharp drops as it winds its way down to Lime Creek which it then follows for a few miles before reconnecting with Hwy. #550. There is good fishing and primitive camping along Lime Creek. Closed in winter, the road provides an excellent cross-country ski trail.

52.0
Cone-shaped Spud Mountain looms ahead and the West Needles are further east. Here is an improved road that leads a short distance to another popular trailhead for ascents of Engineer Mountain.

52.5
It's a long downhill run from the top of Coal Bank Pass to the Animas Valley, which the brakes of heavy trucks often can't handle. Ahead is a gravel ramp which has saved many of these runaway vehicles.

53.1
Between this point and Silverton are numerous avalanche chutes and areas of frequent rock falls. The gate in front of you closes the road in winter when snowplows are unable to keep up with the falling snow, or when avalanches or landslides have blocked the road or made driving hazardous.

54.8
To the southwest you can see the ski runs at Purgatory. The broad, flat-topped mountain slightly more to the west is 12,502 ft. Gray Rock Peak.

56.0
Engineer Mountain is on your left.

56.7
You are now at the summit of 10,640 ft. Coal Bank Pass with a rest area with restrooms, an interpretive sign, and a great place to get out of the car, squash some pine needles between your fingers, and inhale the fragrance of the high country.

An excellent cross-country ski trail, known as the "Power Line" run, begins just across the highway from the rest area and ends several miles below where the highway crosses Cascade Creek. Here a trailhead for Engineer Mountain also provides access to the backcountry and ascents of the popular peak.

In the late 1800's a toll road was built from Silverton to present-day Molas Lake, a little over a mile ahead. At the same time, another wagon road was built from Rockwood to the top of Coal Bank

Hill. These first roads were not connected, and supplies had to be transferred between them on mules. In 1905 the roads were upgraded and connected, providing a complete wagon road between Durango and Silverton. The road was first traversed by automobile in 1920.

57.1

Take advantage of the pull-out just ahead for a view of 13,158 ft. Twilight Peak. Stories are told of a miner who got caught in a snowstorm on his way from Silverton to Durango. Taking refuge under a small overhang, he discovered the largest vein of gold he had ever seen. The sample he took with him on to Durango assayed out as some of the highest quality gold ever found.

Heading back through the canyon to Twilight Peak in the spring, he searched and searched but could never find the ledge again. Many people have searched for this gold in the years since, but the fortune still lies hidden somewhere on its massive slopes.

Grenadier Mountains

57.8

You are approaching a good pullout where you can park and walk back a ways to where a short trail goes to the bottom of a small waterfalls.

59.0

Ahead is a pull-out with an interpretive sign overlooking the old Lime Creek burn, which in 1879 charred 26,000 acres along Lime Creek and the slopes of Coal Bank Hill. The area is still largely barren due to the slow revegetation at this elevation. From here are excellent views of 12,987 ft. Bear Mountain to the north (far left), 13,368 ft. Sultan Mountain to the northeast, and 13,077 ft. Mount Snowdon to the southwest.

59.3

The highway passes over Deer Creek, where there is an easy hiking trail leading a short distance upstream. From here the trail gets more difficult and in a few miles intersects the Cascade Creek and Rico-Silverton trails.

59.6

Below you is the northern end of the Lime Creek road, where you'll find primitive campsites and areas for hiking and picnicking. You can follow this road back south along Lime Creek to where it reconnects with Hwy. #550 at m.m. #51.1 (4WD or all-wheel drive and high clearance vehicles are recommended).

Ahead is the bed of the old road on the slope below the modern highway.

60.4

Just ahead the highway crosses Lime Creek. Twin Sisters Peak (13,432 ft.) is to the northwest.

63.0

Here is an excellent view to the southwest of the sheer north and east faces of Engineer Mountain. The road just ahead leads one-half mile to Andrews Lake, where you will find a restroom, good fishing and more great views. A trail from the lake leads five miles through grassy meadows and forests of spruce and fir to Crater Lake. The trail is easy but long, and offers many good campsites and fine views of Engineer Mountain, Grand Turk, and Twilight Peak.

63.4

To the south is Mount Snowdon.

63.8

Beside the highway on the right is a small pond covered with beautiful yellow lilies in summer and the jagged peaks of the Grenadier Range in the distance. It's hard to see from the highway, but worth stopping for, especially if you are a photographer.

Just ahead, on the summit of Molas Pass at an elevation of 10,910 ft., you are nearly a mile higher than Durango. You are in the Hudsonian Life Zone, which extends from around 10,000 ft. to the upper limits of the spruce and fir forests around 11,500 feet. There is a large pull-out, restrooms, and an interpretive sign.

In the east you can see the Continental Divide, and in every direction more peaks of the San Juans. Covering more than 10,000 square miles, the San Juans are the largest range within the Rocky Mountains south of Alaska. With 13 peaks rising above 14,000 ft., and many others only slightly less, they are also the highest range in the nation. The twin peaks of Grand Turk Mountain (13,087 ft.) can be seen to the north. Further to the east is Sultan Mountain (13,370 ft.), Storm Peak (13,487 ft.), Dome Mountain (13,368 ft.), and Kendall Mountain (13,068 ft.). To the southeast is the Grenadier Range.

The rolling slopes around you are covered in deep snow by mid- January, making this a popular area for cross-country skiing and snowmobiling. Here you are also breathing the cleanest air in the United States--an honor that has been bestowed on Molas Pass. Portions of several movies have been filmed here, including Across the Wide Missouri with Clark Gable and Ricardo Montaban, and Winter Hawk with Leif Erickson and L Q. Jones.

64.1

Just ahead the highway intersects the Colorado Trail. Between Durango and Denver the trail passes through seven national forests, five major river drainages, and crosses the Continental Divide 12 times. Its highest point is 13,271 feet above sea level, and most of the trail is above 10,000 feet.

64.3

The road to the west leads a mile to Little Molas Lake where you will find more good fishing and primitive camping. Just beyond the lake is a great area for wandering below the lofty peaks where endless mountains stretch to the horizon.

65.1

Here you'll find a short road leading to the Molas Lake trailhead which you can follow into the over 400,000 acre Weiminuche Wilderness, the largest in Colorado.

Molas Lake with Grenadiers in background

65.5

To the east, sitting in a basin created by glacial scouring, and with the beautifully rugged Grenadier Range as a backdrop, is Molas Lake Park. A popular hiking and backpacking trail into the Weminuche Wilderness, known as the Snowflake Trail, leaves from the lake and leads to the Animas River and Elk Park.

66.5

Here is a large pull-out with the rugged Grenadier Mountains to the southeast. An old log fence provides a great foreground for photography.

67.0

You are now descending into the Silverton caldera (a large crater formed by the collapse of a volcanic cone). This has been one of the richest mining districts in the world, and much of the wealth of Wall Street once came from fortunes made here.

68.1

The highway crosses Deadwood Gulch where there is a pull-out beside a small but scenic waterfall. Ahead are good locations for photographing Silverton.

70.0

Here is a large pull-out and interpretive sign. Encircled by rugged volcanic peaks lies Silverton, the oldest continuous settlement in the San Juans, and popularly known as the "Silver Queen of Colorado". In the valley to the east is the Animas River and the tracks of the Durango & Silverton Narrow Gauge Railroad as they emerge from the

Animas Gorge. Anvil Mountain rises to the northeast, Storm Peak to the northwest, and Kendall Mountain to the east.

Overview of Silverton

Just past m.m. #70 on the right is an improved road leading to good locations to photograph the train emerging from the Uncomphagre Gorge as it nears Silverton. In just over half a mile is an interpretive sign beside the road. Stop here and watch the train as it approaches. A short distance further down the dirt road is a large abandoned mine. Park here and follow the dirt road a ways and you can see the train bridge over the Animas River on your left. From here you can see a huge boulder that juts into the river, offering a great vantage point to watch the train.

70.2
You are approaching an intersection, with the left branch (U.S. Hwy. #550) continuing on to Ouray, and the right branch (State Highway #110)

leading through downtown Silverton and on up the Animas River Valley towards Animas Forks and Cinnamon and Engineer Passes which lead on to Ouray and Lake City. These roads require 4WD high-clearance vehicles.

The large gray Victorian building just south of the intersection is the visitor's center where you can get a sense of Silverton during the boom days of long-ago. For information call 970-387-5654.

Silverton

Silverton was incorporated in 1876, the same year Colorado became a state. Originally called Baker's Park in honor of Charles Baker, the name was changed to Silverton after the operator of one of the mines, when asked by a reporter from a Denver newspaper if they were finding a lot of gold, boasted that, "We have a lot of gold, but we have silver by the ton." Between 1876 and 1915, thousands of tons of silver ore, as well as hundreds of tons of gold ore, were removed from the surrounding mountains.

San Juan County was a prospector's paradise in those days. Established in 1876 in the heart of the San Juan Mountains, the county comprises 389 square miles of rugged mountain peaks, deep chasms, and high alpine meadows. Superimposed upon this awesome terrain is one of the most remarkable mineralized zones in North America. Mines near Silverton such as the Gold Run, Bear Creek, Sylvanite, and Silvertip produced incredibly rich ore worth up to $44,000 a ton!

Overall, the district has produced 1,500,000 ounces of gold and more than 50,000,000 ounces of silver, lead, and zinc.

Silverton became one of the most famous towns of the old west. Take a walk down Blair Street and recapture a sense of the days when Bat Masterson and Wyatt Earp gambled away their time in some of the 40 saloons and brothels that lined the street. At one time, a two-block section of this busy street employed over 300 dance hall girls in gambling and sporting houses such as the Mikado, Diamond Belle, Sage Hen, Diamond Tooth Lil's, and the Bonton. These and other public buildings like the courthouse, town hall, the Carnegie Library, and the Grand Imperial Hotel, which has had guests such as Lillian Russell, Marilyn Monroe and John F. Kennedy, reflect the architecture of the time.

Downtown Silverton

Unlike most other mining towns, Silverton has never had a major fire, and most of the historic buildings are still standing. The Maverick Queen, with Barbara Stanwick and Barry Sullivan, was filmed here. Today Silverton is recognized as a National Historic District. Visit the San Juan County Museum on the east side of town which is open daily through mid-October and contains exhibits of early-day Silverton and the San Juans.

Follow Greene (Main) Street east through downtown Silverton and head up the Animas Valley. At the edge of town you will see the old cemetery on a hill to your left. A walk through the cemetery provides a good view overlooking Silverton and a good sense of how fragile life was in the early days of the mining town.

A few miles farther, C.R. #4 will take you to the site of Howardsville, an old mining town and the original county seat of San Juan County. Here the road branches off into Cunningham Gulch. Part way up the valley 4WD is required where a branch road leads over Stony Pass, once part of the main road from Durango until the railroad reached Silverton in 1882. Beyond the summit, you can follow the headwaters of the Rio Grande River into the historic mining town of Creede.

At the end of the valley you will find a popular hiking trail taking you through lush forests and meadows of wildflowers into the high country above timberline, and on to the Highland Mary Lakes. Here is good camping and fishing, the usual great views, and connecting trails to the Continental Divide and Colorado Trails.

Twelve miles farther up the Animas Valley above Silverton, at an elevation of 11,200 ft., is the ghost-town of Animas Forks. The town's first log cabin was built in 1873 and by 1883 the town had become a bustling mining community of 450 people. At that time the town contained 30 cabins, a hotel, a general store, a saloon, and a post office. Its population began to decline along with mining activity in the late 1800's, and it was a ghost-town by the 1920's.

Animas Forks Ghost Town above Silverton

The Animas Forks Road is rough and narrow but passable by most cars if caution is used. Beyond here 4WD is required to reach Lake City and Ouray. Prior to 1884, most travel between Silverton and Ouray was by way of Cinnamon and Engineer Passes. In that year, crews working from both directions met at the top of Red Mountain Pass, connecting the two towns by the route of today's highway.

Silverton to Ouray

Continuing along the Skyway from Silverton towards Ouray, head north again on Hwy. #550 from the junction in front of the visitors center. In half-a-mile CR #6 leads to the "Christ of the Mines Shrine", which can be seen on the slopes of Anvil Mountain above Silverton. Carved in Italy from local stone, weighing 12 tons and standing over 12 feet tall, the statue, with outstretched arms as if guarding the town, was erected in 1959 as a tribute to the miners of the San Juans. From the Shrine, there is a wonderful view of Silverton and the surrounding mountains.

To many, this Shrine represents a miracle. At the time of its erection, mining was at an all-time low, with not a single mine operating in the San Juans. There was hope that somehow the Shrine might help revitalize the local economy. Within a few months after its dedication, there was a renewed interest in mining. The Sunnyside Mine, the state's richest gold mine, was re-opened, and one of the most profitable periods in the town's history began.

70.8

Looking south from the Shrine, the spires of the West Needle Mountains rise above the Uncomphagre Gorge. To the east, at the base of Sultan Mountain, are the remains of the old North Star Mine. Discovered in 1879, it is still a major producer of silver.

71.6

Back on Hwy. #550 towards Ouray is another bar-gate used to close the road when heavy snow turns Red Mountain Pass into the country's most treacherous, avalanche prone mountain pass. To the west are South Mineral Creek and South Lookout Peak.

72.0

The South Mineral Creek Road (F.R. #55) leaves the highway here. There are numerous primitive camping places along the stream, and in a little over 2 miles is the Golden Horn N.F.S Campground. About a hundred yards beyond the campground, park your car and listen for the sound of a small waterfall. Find a way through or around the wall of shrubbery and the falls is a short distance ahead. It's worth the effort and is a good location for a photograph.

Water Falls on South Mineral Creek

Watch as you continue following Mineral Creek for a much larger waterfalls on the other side of the creek. It is one of the most beautiful in this area, which will soon come into view from within the hidden cleft it has carved in the canyon wall. The base of the falls can be reached by wading the creek. It's a bit tricky but worth the effort and offers an opportunity for an outstanding photograph.

The main road ends soon at the South Mineral Creek N.F.S. Campground (23 sites). A short distance before the campground a relatively easy 4WD road leads 2 miles to Clear Lake, nestled in a high bowl with stunning turquoise water and surrounded by beautifully rugged mountain peaks. Here you feel the majesty of the San Juans. From the campground, a hiking trail leads a mile-and-a-half to beautiful Ice Lake. The trail is steep but the scenery is gorgeous.

Return to Hwy. #550 and head on towards Ouray

74.3

Across the valley is a good example of an avalanche chute. Powdery snow becomes one of the most destructive forces in nature when it accumulates along the high ridges, then breaks free and comes roaring down the mountainside at tremendous speeds, destroying everything in its path.

75.1

Ahead is San Juan C.R. #8, which leads over 11,700 ft. Ophir Pass. It was originally a pack trail but was upgraded in 1881 to provide a stage and wagon route between Silverton and Ophir. Ophir was named by hopeful prospectors after the biblical location of King Solomon's Mines. Today the 4WD high-clearance road provides a scenic shortcut between Silverton and Telluride.

76.7

Here is a pull-out and an interpretive sign describing the Chattanooga Valley which you are now entering. At the northern end, just before starting up the curving ascent of Red Mountain Pass, are the remains of Chattanooga, which had a population of around 300 in 1883. Quoting from Durango's "Solid Muldoon" newspaper, "The wagon road from Silverton to Chattanooga is dangerous even for pedestrians. The average depth of mud is three feet and the grade is "four parts vertical and one part perpendicular". The arrival of the railroad in the late 1880's was disastrous for the town, which served as a supply station for mines in the area. By the early 1890's, fires and avalanches had destroyed most of the deserted buildings, but a few of the old structures are still standing.

78.4

As you negotiate Mule Shoe curve on the southern slope of Red Mountain, you will see Bear Mountain dominating the view to the south. Below are the remains of the old Silverton Railroad right-of-way.

78.9

Down the slope are the remains of the Silver Ledge Mine, which began producing high-grade silver in 1883.

80.0

Here is the summit of 11,075 ft. Red Mountain Pass, which separates the San Juan and the Uncompahgre National Forests and the watersheds of the Animas River to the south and the Uncompahgre River to the north. The mountains are dotted with old mine shafts, and one can be seen on the east side of the highway just past the interpretive sign. These mines are usually uninteresting tunnels, often filled with water, which soon dead-end. Veins of ore were followed until the ore ran out or it was no longer feasible to continue with the digging. These mines can be dangerous and should not be entered.

Red Mountain

The dramatic soil coloration that gave Red Mountain its name is the result of the oxidation of minerals from the lava rock overlying the area. A short 4WD road leads from the summit to the site of Congress, which had a population of over 100 in 1883. The famous Black Bear Pass road to Telluride heads west from the summit. In the past, there was a sign at the beginning of the road that read "You don't have to be crazy to drive this road, but it helps".

The name "Million Dollar Highway" originated with the 12-mile section of highway between the summit of Red Mountain Pass and Ouray. This is the only section of the highway that was designed and built under the sole supervision of Otto Mears, the famous road builder known as the "Pathfinder of the Rockies".

There are numerous stories about the origin of the highway's name. One suggests that the roadbed is paved with mine tailings containing a fortune in gold and silver ore. Another assumes building costs of a million dollars a mile. And a story is told of a female passenger who told a stagecoach driver, after having ridden a short distance south from Ouray, that she wanted to walk back, saying that she wouldn't travel that road any further for a million dollars.

The less interesting truth is that during a planning meeting in the early 1920's, a comment concerning the cost of construction was made about "this million dollar highway". During the dedication ceremony in July, 1924, it was officially referred to as the "Million Dollar Highway".

Even after the road was opened to automobile traffic, heavy snowfalls kept it closed much of the winter, and it wasn't until 1935 that the road was open year-round. The modern highway, completed in 1955, is still frequently closed by Mother Nature for hours or even days at a time.

80.5

A short 4WD road leads from here to the town sites of Red Mountain and Guston, which can soon be seen across the valley. Red Mountain reached its heyday by 1883, when it had a main street two blocks long and a population of around 600. Nearby Guston had a population of 300 by 1890. Fires and snow have destroyed most of what remained of the towns, but the few buildings still standing make it an interesting place to explore.

81.8

Ahead on the left is the Red Mountain Mining District view-point overlooking the Idarado (Idaho/ Colorado) Mine Complex, where large amounts of gold, copper, lead, and silver have been produced since the 1940's. Red Mountain is to the southeast. The old houses here provided housing for the miners.

82.0

Across the valley, the most visible remains of Guston is the tall shaft house of the Yankee Girl Mine. Along here, just off the highway on the right, several short roads connect decaying buildings associated with the mines along Red Mountain Creek. These old houses, hidden behind the trees, are great to visit and photograph but care is needed to help preserve them.

Yankee Girl Mine

83.5

The old buildings on the other side of Red Mountain Creek are the remains of those associated with the Joker Tunnel. The major mines nearby, the Yankee Girl, Guston, and Robinson, had all been worked to such depths that production costs became prohibitive. These mines were vertical shafts, and the Joker Tunnel was designed as a horizontal tunnel beneath them, enabling the force of gravity to help remove the ore. The shaft house of the Yankee Girl Mine can be seen on the slopes above.

84.8

Ahead is a large tailings pond formed from the processing of ore at the Idarado Mine. The waste from the processing was mixed with water to form a slurry, then pumped into this pond, allowing the residue to settle out.

From the north end of the pond a primitive road parallels it on the west side. In a short distance it passes a foot bridge over Red Mountain Creek where a trail leads up the slope to the Yankee Girl and the site of Guston.

86.0
The term "park" refers to large, open valleys in the high country that are encircled by mountains. Parks are prominent features of the southern Rockies, and you are now in Ironton Park which, like much of the landscape you have been passing through, was created largely by glaciers. In 1890 the town of Ironton, with 10 saloons and 300 cabins, stood at the south end of the park.

87.0
Minerals add an orange color to the waters of Red Mountain Creek, which flows beside the highway. West of the highway is Crystal Lake, which is privately owned but open to the public and is a great early morning or evening location for photographing the reflections of Red Mountain. The 5.6 mile long Hayden Trail begins at the north end of the lake and ends at F.R. #896. There are beautiful views in all directions.

On the east side of the highway are the remains of a once elegant lodge, whose guests included the governor of Colorado at its opening in 1940.

87.4
Here the highway begins its descent into the awesome Uncompahgre Gorge. This is one of the most amazing stretches of highway in North

America, and it is this section that is remembered when people talk of the Million Dollar Highway.

87.9

The memorial here is dedicated to those who have lost their lives in the infamous "Riverside Slide", which crosses the highway just ahead. Until the snowshed was built in 1985, it was the most deadly snowslide in the country. Unseen avalanches descend 3,200 vertical feet before slamming into the highway and the valley below. In the days of stage coach and wagon, it was often necessary to tunnel 600 feet through snow over 70 feet deep to keep the road open.

Avalanches are one of the most powerful forces in nature. Stories are told about a huge snowplow that was swept into the bottom of the canyon by an avalanche and remained entombed in the concrete-like snow until spring. And of a car that, when recovered, was packed full of snow but the windows were closed. The glove compartment was packed with snow, but the door was closed. A flashlight inside the compartment was also packed with snow but the flashlight was undamaged. Like a frail straw of wheat driven deep into a solid fence post by a powerful tornado, the powers of nature are often unbelievable.

89.5

Just ahead, the Uncompahgre River flows under the highway on its way to the bottom of the gorge and the Uncompahgre Valley beyond. Uncompahgre means "hot springs" in the Ute language. Here the 4WD Engineer Pass Road leaves the highway and begins its climb to the

12,800 ft. summit with its vistas of rolling alpine tundra and snow-capped peaks.

The Engineer Pass Road here is part of the scenic Alpine Loop connecting Silverton, Ouray, and Lake City. One of the country's National Scenic Back-Country Byways, it follows the path of the Ute Indians and later adventurers, prospectors, miners and settlers. The road can be followed from here to Lake City, or a spur road connecting the Engineer Pass Road with the Cinnamon Pass Road (12,620 ft.) can be followed to Silverton. Along this route you can immerse yourself in the natural beauty of some of the most spectacular mountain scenery in North America, as well as the nostalgia of ghost towns and abandoned mines.

90.0

You are now in the heart of the Uncompahgre Gorge, where rocks as much as two-and-a-half billion years old are exposed. These formations, which are as old as those in the depths of the Grand Canyon, were laid down during the first episodes of mountain building in pre-Cambrian time and form the foundation of today's Rockies.

On the opposite side of the canyon, clinging to a narrow granite ledge rising high above the foreboding Uncomphagre Gorge, colorfully faded old clothes are sometimes seen waving in the breeze, clinging tenaciously to the decaying old clothes line clinging tenaciously to the decaying old house. "Margaret Weatherly, June 7, 1924", is carved on the door. Nearby a dark, empty tunnel in the granite cliff is all that remains of the once promising Neosha Mine. (The old cabin is maintained by the Ouray Historical Society)

Like hundreds of other mines in these unforgiving mountains, it has its own story of isolation, loneliness, lost opportunity, and sometimes unexpected good fortune in the search for riches in the San Juans. Though no mineral riches were found, one of the most beloved songs in the English language is tied closely to this decaying old shack.

Margaret's brother-in-law, Frederic Weatherly, an English songwriter and lyricist, sent her the words to a song he had written after visiting Ouray, asking for her help with the music. Scottish-born Margaret was familiar with a tune she had heard sung by Scottish miners in Silverton's bars and dancehalls. Adapting the words to the music, she returned it to her brother-in-law, and in 1915 the song "Oh Danny Boy" was released.

90.5
Beside the highway is a memorial to Otto Mears, the "Pathfinder of the Rockies", who is most remembered for the engineering feat seen along this section of highway.

90.6
Just ahead, the highway crosses above Bear Creek Falls as it begins its 227 foot drop into the canyon below. Horsetail Falls is across the gorge, and Mount Abrams dominates the skyline to the south. Just past Bear Creek is a pull-out on the left with interpretive signs and a small platform that extends over the cliff edge for a great view of the falls.

90.8

The highway passes through a short tunnel just ahead. At the south end of the tunnel is a pull-out and the trailhead for the Bear Creek National Recreation Trail which is a hiking trail closed to horses, bicycles, and motor vehicles. A short hike will take you above the highway for a great view of the Uncompahgre Gorge and the valley in the distance. Beyond here, the trail leads two-and-a-half miles to the Grizzly Bear mine and another one-and-a-half miles to the Yellow Jacket Mine. It also serves as another connecting trail leading seven miles to Engineer Mountain.

Grand Mesa, the world's largest flat-topped mountain, can be seen 80 miles north. Rising 6,000 ft. above the surrounding river valleys and reaching a maximum elevation of 11,333 ft., it has an area of about 500 square miles stretching 40 miles east from Grand Junction between the Colorado and Gunnison Rivers. Over 300 lakes are scattered over the top of the formation, and it is a major attraction for outdoor enthusiasts.

92.0

Ahead is a large and easily accessible turn-out overlooking Ouray, named after a famous chief of the Tabeguache band of Ute Indians who once roamed these mountains. The town, sitting in a magnificent volcanic caldera, is a National Historic Landmark often referred to as the "Switzerland of the Rockies".

Ouray

Long ago the Ute Indians discovered this sheltered valley of abundant game, forests, streams and hot springs. The first known white men to see the valley was in 1875 when a small group of prospectors crossed Engineer Pass from the Silverton area. Rich discoveries of silver and gold were soon made, and Ouray's population grew to around 2,000 by 1890. Today, thanks to the Victorian charm of the town, the natural beauty of its surroundings, and the relaxing hot-springs, tourism has replaced mining as the primary revenue producer.

92.2

This road leads to the Amphitheater NFS Campground. Beyond the camping area is a scenic overlook of Ouray and the surrounding mountains. A moderate two-and-a-half mile trail to the top of the cliffs overlooking Ouray and Cascade Falls begins at the campground.

92.8

Ahead is C.R. #361, which leads to Box Canyon Falls, the Camp Bird Mine, and Yankee Boy Basin. For hundreds of thousands of years the waters of Canyon Creek, which you cross shortly after leaving the highway, have been carving this magnificent chasm. An easy and exciting hike along the creek to the base of the roaring falls will give you a sense of intimacy with the sculptured canyon, while a more strenuous trail leads to the High Bridge for a breathtaking view over the falls and into the depths below.

Beyond Box Canyon Falls, C.R. #361 continues on towards the Camp Bird Mine and Yankee Boy Basin. The Camp Bird turned Ouray into a boomtown producing over $26,000,000 in gold and other ores between 1896 and 1910. It also turned Tom Walsh, its discoverer, into one of the world's richest men. Walsh's daughter Evelyn was at one time the owner of the Hope Diamond. The five miles of road to the mine is suitable for passenger cars, but 4WD is required beyond this point.

Yankee Boy Basin is an alpine basin well known for its amazing display of summer wild flowers framed by the 14,000 ft. peaks of the Sneffels Range, and for beautiful Twin Falls on Sneffels Creek. Access is by a four-wheel drive road which twists and turns through stunning country as it climbs upward.

Sitting in a stunningly beautiful valley a quarter-mile wide and half-a-mile long, Ouray is truly a "Gem of the Rockies". Prospectors first arrived in the area in 1875 and gold veins were soon found in Imogene Basin just east of town. Incorporated in 1876, the town soon grew to a population of over a thousand and became the county seat of the newly formed Ouray County. At the height of the mining, Ouray had more than 30 active mines.

Ouray's entire Main Street is a registered National Historic District with most of the buildings including the Ouray County Courthouse, St. Elmo Hotel, St. Joseph's Miner's Hospital, the Western Hotel, and Wright's Opera House dating to the late nineteenth century.

Historic Beaumont Hotel--Downtown Ouray

For a glimpse of yesterday, visit the Ouray County Historical Museum located two blocks east of Main Street on 6th Avenue. You can also enjoy the half mile trail to the base of Cascade Falls that begins at the upper end of 8th Avenue.

94.0

Here is an opportunity to relax in the hot waters of a spring-fed public pool. Ouray offers an abundance of outdoor activities. More information is available at the visitor's center located beside the pool, or call 800-228-1876.

Ouray to Ridgeway

From Ouray, the Skyway continues north on U. 5.Highway #550 towards Ridgway.

95.1

The City of Ouray Rotary Park is a day-use area with shady picnic sites, tables, water, and restrooms.

95.4

The highway crosses Dexter Creek, which originates a few miles east below Bighorn Ridge, and joins the Uncompahgre River west of the highway. Lake Lenore is about a quarter-of-a-mile east. From there, a hiking trail (#216) can be followed past the remains of the Old Maid Mine and into the backcountry of the Big Blue Wilderness below Cimarron Ridge. Within four miles trail #216 intersects trail #217, which follows Cutler Creek for a few miles before rejoining trail #216 at Lake Lenore for a loop hike of about 10 miles.

98.3

Cutler Creek originates about three miles east, and joins the Uncompahgre River just west of the highway. Like the Animas Valley near Durango, this sheltered valley has been an important feeding area for big-game animals and other wildlife for thousands of years. Winter is a good time for observing and photographing the large herds of elk that gather here.

99.1

The old Ouray Cemetery is beside the highway here. To the south, Mount Abrams dominates the skyline above Ouray.

100.0

News of fertile valleys like this along the Uncompahgre River attracted many homesteaders, farmers, and ranchers to the San Juans. Barbed wire was first used in these mountains in 1878, and by the early 1880's, the days of the open range were quickly becoming a memory.

102.2

At clothing-optional Orvis Hot Springs, just off the highway on C.R. #3, you can enjoy a wonderful outdoor spring-fcd hot pool, a large indoor pool, hot-tubs, and saunas.

In 1919, the Orvis family who owned the springs and surrounding land, first opened the springs for commercial use, calling it the "Orvis Plunge". There are numerous natural hot-springs dotting the valley between Ouray and Ridgway. In winter, when clouds of steam from these warm waters rise into the air, and herds of elk and deer wander the open meadows, it's easy to see why this protected valley had been a favorite refuge of the Ute Indians for centuries.

103.0

Just ahead is the junction of U. S. Hwy. #550 and #62. The Skyway turns west here through Ridgway towards Telluride on Hwy. #62. The Ridgway Visitor Center is located at the junction of these two highways. For information call 970-626-5181.

For a wonderful one or two-day trip, drive north on Hwy. #550 from this junction for a couple of miles, then turn east on C.R. #10, which leads to F.R. #858. This road is a little rough but fine for most passenger cars. There are great views of Courthouse Mountain, which often turns red at sunset, at m.m. #8, and more stunning views as you near 11,120 ft. Owl Creek Pass. Just over the pass are the jagged peaks of Turret and Pinnacle Ridges. Silver Jack Reservoir, known for its beautiful scenery, camping, and fishing, lies another six miles ahead.

Courthouse Mountain

Beyond the reservoir, F.R. #858 passes the Beaver Lake (11 sites) and Big Cimarron (16 sites) NFS Campgrounds before intersecting Hwy. #50 at the Curecanti National Recreation Area. From here it's only 12 miles west to the Black Canyon of the Gunnison National Monument, then just a few more miles to Montrose, where you can reconnect with Hwy. #550 and head back to Ridgway. Another nearby point-of-interest located a few miles north of this junction on Hwy. #550 is Ridgway State Park where you'll find 1,000-acre Ridgway Reservoir. It's a great place for boating, camping and fishing.

Ridgway to Placerville

Turn west on Hwy. #62 just ahead and you'll soon be in downtown Ridgway, named after R.M. Ridgway, first superintendent of the Rio Grande Southern Railroad. Incorporated in 1891, it began as a junction on the Rio Grande Southern's narrow-gauge route, which covered terrain so rugged that 130 bridges were needed to negotiate the 165 miles from here through Rico to Durango. Along with the railroad came ranching, and Ridgway soon grew into a typical western cowtown with five saloons and horse races down Main Street.

Galloping Goose

It was here that master mechanic Jack Odenbaugh and his brother Walter constructed the first "Galloping Goose "in 1931 from the body of a Buick "Master Six" four-door sedan. These railcars were much lighter and less expensive for the Rio

Grande Southern to build and operate than the steam locomotives, and seven "geese" were built in the railroad's shops in Ridgway. First used for carrying mail, they were later used to carry tourists, and the name "Galloping Goose" became officially recognized by the railroad.

Enjoy the shady city park as you imagine the excitement when John Wayne walked through the swinging doors of the old saloon across the street (now the "True Grit" cafe) during the filming of True Grit and How the West was Won.

22.0
The Skyway now continues west from Ridgway towards Placerville. Mt. Sneffels and the Sneffels Range are to the south.

22.4
Here's the road to "Log Hill Village". During the 1880's, freight haulers found the going tough as they descended with their teams and wagons into the spectacular Uncompahgre Valley from the high mesa to the north. They would drag a heavy log behind the wagons to slow the descent. The mesa thus became known as "Log Hill".

19.5
The improved East Dallas Creek Road (C.R. #7) leaves the highway here and heads south towards the Sneffels Range. This road splits less than two miles after leaving the highway, with the left fork, which follows Beaver Creek, turning into a 4WD road in about two miles, then ending in a couple more miles after crossing the national forest boundary below Whitehouse Mountain.

The right fork is an improved road which crosses into the national forest in about four miles, providing access to primitive campsites along the East Fork of Dallas Creek before reaching the Blue Lakes trailhead at Willow Swamp. This is a popular hike to three scenic lakes in a beautiful glacial basin surrounded by rugged summits including Mount Sneffels (14,150 ft.), Dallas Peak (13,809 ft.), and Gilpin Peak (13,694 ft.). From here the trail gets more difficult as it climbs over Blue Lakes Pass into Yankee Boy Basin near Ouray.

18.9
The improved West Dallas Road (C.R. #9) follows the West Fork of Dallas Creek for about six miles before crossing the national forest boundary and ending in Box Factory Park. Along the way you'll intersect the Dallas trail, which is a hiking trail that connects with the Blue Lakes Trail about two miles east. The scenery along the drive is spectacular.

16.0
You are now starting up the eastern slope of the Dallas Divide.

Sneffels Range from Dallas Divide

13.7

Here is one of the most photographed scenes in the Rocky Mountains. From here, 14,150 ft. Mount Sneffels dominates the view to the south. The mountain was named after a passage in Jules Vern's Journey to the Center of the Earth in which he depicts a volcanic Mount Sneffels in Iceland as the entrance to the earth's core. Interestingly, Navajo legend says it was from these rugged mountains that the Dineh, "The People", emerged into this world from another world inside the earth.

To the right of Mount Sneffels are Dallas (13,809 ft.) and Campbell (13,213 ft.) mountains. To the left are Cirque Mountain (13,686 ft.), Mount Ridgway (13,468 ft.), and Whitehouse Mountain (13,375 ft.). Further to the east is the Courthouse Range and Cimarron Ridge. Peaks in the West Elk Mountains near Crested Butte can be seen in the distance to the northeast.

In December, 1848, mistakenly thinking that these mountains could be crossed in winter, an expedition led by Colonel John C. Fremont and the famous mountain man, Bill Williams, headed west into the San Juans from the San Luis Valley, a hundred miles east. They soon became stranded in snows over ten feet deep and temperatures of twenty degrees below zero. Ten men and 120 mules were lost in what is considered one of the worst disasters in the exploration of the west. Fremont later described the San Juans as "the highest, most rugged, most impracticable and inaccessible of the Rocky Mountains".

13.4

This is the summit of the Dallas Divide, and the San Miguel/Ouray county line. The Dallas Divide Road was opened in 1882 as another of Otto Mears toll roads, and was later the route used by his narrow-gauge railroad. The first train made it from Durango, over the divide, and on to Ridgway on December 21, 1891. In the early 1900's, the first automobile to cross the Dallas Divide from Ridgway to Placerville made the 22 mile trip in 15 hours.

12.7

Last Dollar Road (F.R. #638) heads south here and, after passing through grassy meadows, magnificent aspen groves, and past rustic old homesteads, connects in 25 miles with Hwy. #145 near Telluride. Along the way are pleasant N.F.S. campsites and beautiful views of the Sneffels and San Miguel Mountains. This is an improved road which is fine for higher clearance 4WD/all-wheel drive vehicles but is not recommended for regular passenger cars.

10.0

At an elevation of 9,000 feet, you are again in the Canadian Life Zone. Aspens, which are common in the valley and on the surrounding slopes, are the most abundant and widely distributed trees in North America. They prefer open, sunny slopes and are among the first trees to repopulate areas ravaged by fire.

6.0

Leopard Creek parallels the highway between the Dallas Divide and Placerville. Here, you are at an elevation of 8,000 ft. As you drop in elevation heading west, the aspens along the creek are being replaced by their close relative the cottonwood, whose fall display of colors rival that of the aspen.

5.7

Lone Cone (12,613 ft.), one of the western-most peaks of the San Juans, towers over the ridge ahead of you.

2.4

This pull-out provides easy access to Leopard Creek.

Placerville to Telluride

1.0

Just ahead is the junction of U.S. Highways #62 & #145.

Here the Skyway turns southeast on Hwy. #145 towards Telluride. In less than a mile you'll come to m.m. #84 just before Placerville. The San Miguel county park ahead is a day-use area with shaded picnic tables, water, and restrooms.

Placerville was founded as a gold mining town in 1877, and named for the area's placer mines. Most mining in the San Juans was "hard rock" mining, but the gravels of the San Miguel River near here contained a treasure in gold washed down from the surrounding mountains. The gold was recovered by sifting the gravel in long troughs with running water, much as with gold-panning.

Originally located half-a-mile west, below the junction of the San Miguel River and Leopard Creek, the town was rebuilt in its present location after storms in 1909 sent Leopard Creek roaring out of its banks, destroying the town. The new town was first known as "Dry Diggings", then as "Hangtown", before being renamed Placerville.

82.7

The improved Fall Creek Road (F.R. #618) heads south eight miles to Woods Lake. Sitting below the towering peaks of the Wilson Mountains, this is a popular fishing lake where you'll find a N.F.S. campground (25 sites). Connecting roads lead to Lone Cone and beyond, eventually reaching Dunton and Hwy. # 145 near Rico. Hiking trails from the lake lead into Navajo Basin and the Lizard Head Wilderness.

The colorful cliffs in this section of the San Miguel Canyon are sedimentary sandstones of the Colorado Plateau which butts up against the Rocky Mountain's western slopes. Near the Utah border to the west, the San Miguel joins the Dolores River, and together they have cut an incredible red rock canyon that meets the Colorado River just north of Moab, Utah.

81.4

A primitive road where you'll find a couple of campsites and access to some good fishing holes leaves the highway here and parallels the river to the edge of Sawpit. An old footbridge still spans the river beside the aging mining structure just off the highway.

80.0

Sawpit, at an elevation of 7,554 ft., was incorporated in 1896 with a population of 36. The name came from the numerous "sawpits" which were located in the area. These pits were large holes dug in the ground over which a log was placed for cutting. Using a huge saw, a team of two men worked with one man in the hole and the other on the ground above.

78.6

The Silver Pick Road (F.R. #622) is an improved road heading up Big Bear Creek, then turning into a 4WD road leading into the national forest and on into Silver Pick Basin. Here you'll find some interesting old mining structures, and hiking trails leading into the Lizard Head Wilderness below El Diente, Gladstone, and Mt. Wilson.

On the opposite side of the highway is the foundation of the Vanadium Mill, which was built in the early 1900's and produced the uranium used in the first atomic bomb. A "Beware of Radiation" sign is its only memorial.

75.0
A Forest Service sign here indicates a road into Deep Creek. On the south side of the highway maintenance building is the other end of the river access road that reconnects with the highway at m.m. #80.8.

This improved road drops into the San Miguel Valley near the site of the old railroad station of Vance Junction, then follows the South Fork of the San Miguel for a few miles before re-connecting with highway # 145 near Ophir. This is a typical U-shaped valley formed by the movement of ancient glaciers. There are some nice campsites along the river. As the road climbs out of the south end of the valley, a small white arrow marks the way to the historic Ames Hydroelectric Plant. There's a nice view of the plant as you near the junction with Hwy. #145.

74.0
Here is a sign for Illium Road and NF access for the South Fork Road. Soon you'll see, from left to right, Silver Mountain and the Ophir Needles, and you'll soon see Sheep Mountain, Sunlight Mountain, and Wilson Peak

73.9

The Keystone Overlook has interpretive displays and great views of Wilson Peak and the Sneffels Range above Telluride. A National Forest Sign here tells you that you are entering the Uncomphagre National Forest.

Telluride

72.5

Hwy. #145 turns south towards Dolores, with a spur leading three miles to Telluride. On long-ago Sunday afternoons, Telluride's "carriage set" would drive from town to this point and back, bestowing on the junction the name "Society Turn". If you're continuing into Telluride, Last Dollar Road intersects the highway just beyond of this junction.

Telluride, the "City of Gold", sits in a beautiful canyon at the head of the San Miguel River, surrounded by rugged peaks towering to over

14,000 feet. At the head of the valley is 365 ft. Bridal Veil Falls, the highest in Colorado. At the top of the falls are the remains of the old hydroelectric plant that served the famous Smuggler-Union Mine.

Originally called Columbia, the town owes its name to the rare sulphur-like element known as tellurium which is found locally in the gold ore. Apparently it was sometimes referred to by another name. There's a story of a conductor on the Rio Grande Southern who, due to the harrowing ride through the mountains, liked to yell out "To Hell You Ride" as the train neared town.

In 1875, John Fallon staked the Ajax, Ausboro, Emerald, and Sheridan claims in the valley. That same year, when a ton of ore worth $2,000 was shipped from the Smuggler-Union Mine to the smelter at Alamosa, the rush to Telluride began. Over 300 miles of tunnels were dug into the surrounding mountains to serve mines such as the Liberty Bell, Tomboy, Black Bear, Smuggler, Cimarron, Bullion, and Hidden Treasure. Some of these mines have vertical depths of nearly 3,000 feet, and horizontal tunnels approaching seven miles in length. Over $350,000,000 in ore has been taken from this valley, and most of this is based on the price of gold during the heyday of mining, which was about $20 an ounce!

Here, on the morning of June 24, 1889, Butch Cassidy (George Leroy Parker) pulled his first big robbery when he and the McCarty gang took $10,000 from the San Miguel Valley Bank and headed west towards the notorious bandit hideout of Brown's Park in the badlands of Utah.

Shortly after the arrival of the railroad in 1891, Telluride's population jumped to 4,000. The New Sheridan Hotel, built in 1895 and still a Telluride landmark, was one of finest in the country for sheer elegance and dining. The town also boasted 26 saloons and 12 bordellos.

Telluride, today a National Historic Landmark, offers a variety of outdoor activities and year-round festivals. Check the visitor's center at m.m. #3 on the west side of town (888-605-2578) and the museum on 1st street. One of the original "Galloping Geese" can be seen downtown on Colorado Avenue, and the town park is on the east end of town by the river.

Telluride to Rico and Dolores

Back to the junction with Hwy. #145, The Skyway now continues towards Rico and Dolores

70.0
A road to the Telluride Ski area intersects the highway here. This is one of the finest ski areas in the country, consisting of over 1,000 acres with 62 trails ranging in difficulty from beginner to expert. Snowfall averages over 300 inches per year on the mountain, which boasts a vertical drop of over 3,500 feet.

69.4
Here is a small pull-out and a sign pointing out Sunshine Mountain and Wilson Peak.

67.0
Ahead are the spectacular Ophir Needles, and the small pond on the left is a great location for a photograph. Just ahead is the Sunshine NFS Campground with 15 sites. The west side of the campground offers great views of, from the far left, Silver Mountain, the Ophir Needles, Sheep Mountain, Sunlight Mountain, and the Wilsons. This is a great spot for sunrise!

Ophir Needles

67.9

The discovery of gold and silver in the mountains above you in 1877 led to the founding of Alta, which today is one of the best preserved ghost-towns in the San Juans. It's three miles to the town. The improved road is narrow in places, but suitable for most vehicles except larger motor homes and trailers. Alta Lakes, where you will find plenty of primitive campsites, good fishing, and more Rocky Mountain views, lies a short distance beyond the town.

66.0

The 800 ft. cliffs across the canyon from this pull-out were formed by an intrusion of igneous rock which lifted the overlying layers of Dakota sandstone high above its normal level. To the south, the pinnacles of the Ophir Needles are composed of volcanic and sedimentary rocks which were tipped up vertically by this same intrusion, and which have since eroded into the forms you see today. To the right of the Ophir Needles are Yellow Mountain, Sheep Mountain, Sunshine Mountain, and Wilson Peak.

On the opposite canyon wall you can see the bed of Otto Mear's narrow gauge railroad. The climb out of this canyon presented one of the most difficult obstacles on the route, and it was here that the famous "Ophir Loop" was built, where the trestles looped back over themselves to climb the cliffs.

Just ahead, an improved road drops quickly into the South Fork Valley and connects with Hwy. # 145 south of Telluride. Out of sight below you is the little village of Ames, and the world's first alternating current generating plant. Until the 1880's, all electrical systems had been direct current. Invented by Thomas Edison, this power system was inefficient for distribution over long distances. Alternating current was theoretically more efficient, but its use had never been commercially demonstrated, and experts like Edison didn't think it would work.

A small hydroelectric plant was built at Ames in 1890 by George Westinghouse and Telluride resident L. L. Nunn. Water was channeled out of nearby Trout Lake through the Ilium Flume and piped down a vertical cliff to power the plant, from which a three mile long, 3,000 volt power line was run to the Gold King Mine at Ophir. Its success rang in a new era of electrical transport, and soon lines were supplying other mines long distances away. The little plant is still producing electricity, and the name we are familiar with today is Westinghouse instead of Edison Electric.

On the east side of the highway is a road leading into the town of Ophir, and on over Ophir Pass at the head of the valley. This 4WD road crosses the mountains between Lookout Peak (13,661 ft.) and South Lookout Peak (13,357 ft.), connecting with highway #550 near Silverton. The old Ophir Mill is located just past the turn into the town. During the 1890's, the mill processed nearly $20,000,000 in precious metals which the Gold King Mine's two-mile-long Black Hawk Tunnel removed from the Alta vein.

The old town cemetery is located a couple of miles above town on the north side of the road, though it can't be seen from the road and may take a little looking.

Above Ophir, many glacially polished and striated rocks can be seen in the surrounding cliffs. Because of their smaller size and the hardness of the underlying rocks, the glaciers that occupied this valley were unable to carve downward as rapidly as the larger South Fork glacier in the valley below, leaving this valley high above the San Miguel River after the last glaciers retreated.

64.6

A pull-out here offers great views of the South Fork Valley and the Ilium Flume can be seen across the canyon and in the valley below.

64.0

The 4WD road across the highway on the west drops rapidly through aspen groves and around sharp cliffs to a three-way fork in the road. The left two forks lead to some interesting old mines, and the right fork leads to spectacular views of the falls at the head of the canyon.

63.5
Here is the Matterhorn N.F.S. Campground (28 sites).

62.0
The North Trout Lake Road leads to private homes beside the lake. There are no public services. Sheep Mountain dominates the skyline in the south.

Early Spanish explorers no doubt visited Trout Lake, but the first recorded visit by Europeans was in 1833 when 60 men from the St. Louis Fur Company spent the summer here trapping beaver and other fur-bearing animals. An ancient landslide created the lake from which flow the headwaters of the South Fork of the San Miguel River. Towering above the lake are, from left to right, Yellow Mountain, Pilot Knob, Golden Horn, Vermillion Peak, and Sheep Mountain.

60.3
Just ahead is the 10,222 ft. summit of Lizard Head Pass, where winter snowdrifts are often 20 feet deep. Thousands of years before the first Europeans arrived, Native Americans were using this route to cross between the valleys of the Dolores River, which flows south, and the San Miguel which flows north. Here is a large turn-out with interpretive signs, picnic tables, and restrooms.

The San Miguel rises near Telluride and joins the Dolores 15 miles east of the Utah border. The

Rio de Nuestra Senora de Dolores (The River of Our Lady of Sorrows), which drains a rugged and arid region of the Colorado Plateau west of the San Juan Mountains, was named by 86 year old Juan Maria Antonio Rivera, mentioned earlier, who was the leader of a 1775 treasure hunting expedition from Santa Fe. From here the combined waters of the San Miguel and the Dolores flow west, eventually joining the Colorado River near Moab, and from there on to the Sea of Cortez.

The pass is also the boundary between the Uncompahgre and San Juan National Forests, and San Miguel and Dolores counties. A fairly difficult hiking trail begins here and rises nearly 2,000 feet within three miles as it winds through spruce and fir forests on its way to the summit of Blackface at 12,147 feet. Beyond here, the views are outstanding as the trail continues on to Lizard Head and the 14,000 ft. peaks beyond.

In the 1880's longhorn cattle grazed these high meadows, but by the early 1900's most cattle had been replaced by sheep, which were more adaptable to the mountain climate. The animals were brought into the mountains in the spring and allowed to roam free until fall, when they were rounded up and moved to lower elevations. These round-ups often included as many as half-a-million head of livestock. The pens south of the highway were used to load the animals into rail cars until 1951 when the railroad was shut down. To the southwest are the Rico Mountains, which were named by the early Spanish in whose language "rico" means "rich".

F. R. #626, south of the highway, heads east and in a little over a mile connects with F.R. #627, a 4WD road leading back along the north side of Trout Lake, reconnecting with Hwy. # 145 at m.m. #62.6.

59.6
Pull-outs here offer panoramic views of, from right to left, Sheep Mountain, Vermillion Peak, Golden Horn, Pilot Knob, and Yellow Mountain. The ridge above the highway to the north is "Blackface" and Lizard Head is to its left. Many of these peaks were named by the 1874 Hayden Expedition, a U.S. Geological survey team sent to collect scientific data in the area.

58.4
The Cross Mountain trail heads towards the base of Lizard Head and the East Fork Trail heads south for 11 miles before connecting with other trails near Cahone.

Towards the west, volcanic, or igneous rock is covered by thousands of feet of sediment, but buckling and tilting of the earth's crust pushed today's mountain region high above the surrounding country. Then erosion, much of it due to great glaciers 15,000 years ago, ground away the overlying sediments and carved the harder volcanic materials into today's rugged peaks. This process is seen clearly on Sheep Mountain, whose smooth western slopes are Cretaceous shale from ancient seas, while the peaks are volcanic in origin.

The 20-mile long Galloping Goose Trail, directly across from Lizard Head, follows an old rail line built in 1890 to haul precious metals from these mountains to the smelter in Durango. Crossing a 10,200 ft. pass between Telluride and Durango, this trail passes through some of the state's most beautiful scenery.

58.5

Lizard Head Peak (13,113 ft.) was named by early mountain men, but it lost its resemblance to a lizard long ago when part of the rock fell. To the left of Lizard Head is Cross Mountain (12,703 ft.), Mt. Wilson (14,246 ft.), Gladstone Peak (13,913 ft.), and El Diente (14,159 ft.). These are some of the most difficult mountains in Colorado to climb. Surrounding the peak is the 41,496 acre Lizard Head Wilderness, which straddles both the San Juan and Uncompahgre National Forests. Wilderness designation means that the area is protected in its natural state, and only foot traffic (human, horse, llama, etc.) is allowed.

Lizard Head Peak

F. R. #424, which begins beside the sign pointing out Lizard Head Peak, leads about half-a-mile to the Cross Mountain and Groundhog trailheads, then continues as a 4WD road along the slopes, offering primitive campsites and access to the backcountry. F. R. #424-A, which splits from F.R. #424 shortly after leaving the highway, also wanders up the slopes in the direction of Lizard Head, offering primitive camping and opportunities to wander in a wilderness setting below the lofty peaks.

F. R. #204, across the highway, is a 4WD road which forks shortly, with the right fork ending in half-a-mile in a lovely meadow where some old railroad buildings still stand. From here, the East Fork hiking trail heads south along the headwaters of the Dolores River towards Tin Can Basin and Bolam Pass. The left fork of F.R. #204 wanders through the forest where you'll find primitive campsites and room to roam.

57.9
Here the Dolores River emerges from its hidden origin in the mountains to the south. Snow Spring Creek parallels the highway between here and Lizard Head Pass. Elliott Mountain (12,340 ft.) dominates the skyline just ahead.

Dolores River Canyon

55.0

Elliott Mt. (12,340 ft.) dominates the skyline to the south towards Rico. To the north is Sheep Mountain.

54.0

Just ahead, F.R. #535 leaves the highway, climbs quickly out of the canyon, and heads west through rolling meadows and forests of aspen and pine towards its reconnection in 32 miles with Hwy. #145.

#24.5, 13 miles northeast of Dolores. RV's and larger trailers should access this road at m.m. #24.5.

This improved road closely parallels the excellent trout fishing waters of the West Dolores River. There are great views in all directions and lots of primitive camping. It's eight miles to the Burrow Bridge N.F.S Campground (15 sites), and another two miles to the historic town of Dunton, which began in 1892 as a small mining settlement. It was named after Horatio Dunton who owned several of the hot springs in the area. Dunton is now privately owned.

The West Dolores Campground (13 sites) is another 14 miles west of Dunton. You then pass the Mavresso (14 sites) and Emerson (3 individual sites, 1 group site) Campgrounds in the next eight miles before F.R. #535 rejoins Hwy. # 145 twelve miles east of Dolores.

This road provides access to several trails leading into the backcountry. One of the most popular is the Navajo Lake Trail, which begins a mile south of Burrow Bridge and leads into spectacular Navajo Basin, where spur trails provide routes to the summits of El Diente, Mount Wilson, and Gladstone Peak.

A ways further, N.F. #578 takes you across the river to the large and shady Cayton NFS Campground (27 sites). The road then continues on as a 4WD road to connect in about six miles with the Hermosa Creek Road at Bolam Pass, and then with Hwy. #550 near Purgatory. The Barlow

Creek Trail also begins across the creek and heads over Bolam Pass towards Purgatory.

53.3

Here the highway crosses Coal Creek. Seventy million years ago, during the Cretaceous Period, Southwest Colorado was covered by dense fern forests reaching heights of 100 feet. The organic matter that built up on the ground below these huge forests was eventually covered by sand and mud as the ancient seas rolled in again. The tremendous pressure of this overlying sediment transformed the organic matter into the rich coal beds found here today. There are several primitive campsites along this section of river.

52.4

Part of the old trestle of the Rio Grande Southern still stands beside the river on the south side of the highway.

51.9

The La Plata Mountains west of Durango can be seen down the valley to the south.

49.0

Here the old railroad bed is plainly visible across the river. As more and more silver strikes were made, the mountains became known as the "Silvery San Juans", and the route you are traveling, today's San Juan Skyway, was called the "Silver Circle". Later, as more gold was discovered, the route was referred to as the "Golden Circle". Today's highway roughly follows the route of the Rio Grande Southern, which was built to carry the huge amounts of silver and gold ore from the numerous mines to the smelter in

Durango. Between 1890 and 1891, so much ore was mined along this route that even the railroads couldn't move it fast enough.

48.5
Here the highway crosses the Dolores River just before entering Rico. Ahead is the San Juan National Forest information office.

On the north side of the highway beside Silver Creek is the old shaft-house of the Atlantic Cable Mine. Discovered in 1878, its ore produced 10-15 ounces of silver per ton. It also produced large amounts of lead and zinc ore during World War II.

Rico

Welcome to downtown Rico. When trappers from the St. Louis Fur Company, led by Colonel William Wallen, visited this area in 1823, remains of old smelters showed that the Spanish had lived and mined here much earlier. Rich veins of silver were discovered in 1879, and a new town was born. First called Carbon City, then Carbonateville, then Lead City, then Dolores City, the name Rico was finally decided on. The town soon had 29 buildings including seven saloons, and the census included 58 women among its population of 894.

It was said at the time that anywhere a hole was dug in the ground, a town would spring up. Rico appeared so suddenly that a Telluride newspaper commented that the town "had gotten there before it was sent for". Rico's population peaked in 1892 when it became an important link in the Rio Grande Southern's route with an engine house and depot. Mines such as the Black Hawk and Enterprise each shipped five rail cars of ore per day (each car carried 10 tons) to the smelters in Durango. Take time to see the courthouse and other old buildings and nearby mines.

47.4

A large primitive camping area is located here by the river. Ahead is the old Rico cemetery, with many tombstones dating from the days of the valley's earliest white settlers.

46.0

To the north, Dolores Mountain dominates the skyline. If you look carefully you might see some old rock structures on the other side of the river which are the remains of coke ovens that were part of an early smelting process.

45.7

Just ahead is Scotch Creek and F.R. #550. This 4WD road heads east several miles, connecting with the Hermosa Creek Road at Hotel Draw, then heading over Bolam Pass and eventually connecting with Hwy. #550 at Purgatory.

Quoting from a forest service sign at the beginning of the road: "Rico had the mineral wealth but lack of a reliable transportation route was preventing its development as a mining center. In the late 1870's the Pinkerton Trail through Scotch Creek to the Animas Valley north of Durango provided the initial solution. In 1882 it was replaced with the Scotch Creek Toll Road. Hauling heavy loads was a slow and difficult undertaking. One freighter recorded that he took 35 days and 22 yoke of oxen to haul two steam boilers from Rockwood to Rico, a distance of only 35 miles. When the Rio Grande Southern Railroad reached Rico in 1891 the Scotch Creek route lost its importance. The present Scotch Creek Road uses the toll road right of way. Remains of the Pinkerton Trail can be seen in places cutting through the rocky slopes on the north side of the road.

43.0

There are several primitive campsites beside the river. Here is the Dolores/Montezuma County line and a large area on the river for primitive camping. The Wildcat Trail (#207) crosses the river here, providing access to open, grassy campsites suitable for RV's. This road rejoins the highway in less than a mile.

42.4

This is the south access to the Wildcat Trail mentioned above.

41.9

The Tenderfoot Hiking Trail, which is closed to all motorized vehicles, begins on the north side of the highway beside the pond. It connects with the Calico Trail in four miles, as well as with other trails leading into the Rico Mountains and the Lizard Head Wilderness.

39.4

F.R # 435 is an improved road which follows Roaring Fork Creek for several miles before connecting with F.S. #564. It then heads northeast a few more miles, closely paralleling a segment of the Colorado Trail, eventually connecting with the 4WD Scotch Creek Road.

38.1

To the northeast are the Rico Mountains, whose highest peaks are Dolores Mountain (12,112 ft.), Blackhawk Mountain (12,681 ft.), and Whitecap Mountain (12,335 ft.). Through the gate on the west side of the highway is a primitive campsite and the Schoolhouse Trailhead, which leads about a mile up Schoolhouse Draw.

Mountains above Rico

38.9

The Hillside Drive Road (F.R. #436) is an improved road that heads southeast for several miles, eventually ending below Indian Ridge. There the Colorado Trail follows as it heads north from Kennebec Pass towards its junction with the Highline Trail about 10 miles west of Purgatory. A short trail connects the end of F.R. #436 to the Colorado Trail. From here it's only about five miles south along the Colorado Trail to the La Platas, just west of Durango, and the hike is spectacular.

There is a large area on the river for primitive camping just across the bridge.

36.5

Here is Priest Creek and the trailheads for Priest Gulch and the Calico Trail, both of which head northeast towards Storm and Calico Peaks in the Rico Mountains.

34.1

The Bear Creek and Morrison trailheads are just across the river at the site of the old Wallace ranch, where the road ends. The Bear Creek trail heads southeast into a beautiful sub-alpine valley, becoming more difficult as it continues on towards the La Plata Mountains. In about eight miles it connects with the Highline Trail, which you can follow over Kennebec Pass and into La Plata Canyon west of Durango. Along Bear Creek you'll find several miles of good fishing and a sense of seclusion.

The Morrison trail heads southwest and soon climbs out of the Dolores Valley, reaching the mesa top at 9,785 ft. in a little over two miles. From here it heads into the area east of the La Platas where it links with other interconnecting trails.

30.4

The Taylor Creek Road (F.R. #545) is an improved road that heads northeast about 15 miles towards the western slopes of the Rico Mountains. It follows Taylor Creek most of the way, and you'll find lots of room for camping, fishing and exploring. A couple of side roads that leave

F.S. #545 on the west end in a few miles on the east side of Haycamp Mesa.

28.5

Here is the trailhead for the Loading Pen Hiking Trail. In a little over three miles it crosses the head of Pipe Creek and connects with F.R. #201, which is a branch of F.R. #545 mentioned above.

27.0

The thousand-foot high slickrock walls of the Dolores Canyon here are composed largely of Entrada sandstone, formed during Jurassic times from floodplains, tidal flats, estuaries, and sand dunes. Remains of ancient Anasazi dwellings, the Indians of the Mesa Verde, can be found in alcoves along these cliffs.

26.3

Here is Stoner Creek, the Stoner Lodge and Stoner Creek Campground. Stoner, established in 1890, was named after the rocky creek where it is located, which has been called "Stoner" by locals since 1888.

24.4

Here is the southern end of F.R. #535. A sign says Dunton and West Dolores Road. Check m.m. #54.0 on p. 58 for a description of the recreational opportunities along this road.

12.0

The La Plata Mountains near Durango loom above the valley to the east.

Welcome to Dolores

In the mid 1880's, a town had begun at a place called Big Bend, several miles downstream. When the Rio Grande Southern laid its tracks down the Dolores River Canyon from Ridgway, it was here where they turned south into Lost Canyon towards Mancos. The new town of Dolores sprang up at this junction.

In 1893 the Rio Grande Southern Hotel, which is today a Bed & Breakfast, was built near the railroad depot, and by 1897 there were 200 residents. Dolores didn't have the mineral riches of other towns along the route, but the cattle business was so good that in one year the local bank recorded the highest per capita deposits in the U.S.

Old Dolores Train Station

The old train depot on Railroad Avenue (Hwy. #145) today houses the visitor center and museum. Don't miss one of the two remaining "Galloping Geese", which can be seen near the Visitor Center. These strange gasoline powered railroad "locomotives" for 20 years carried passengers and mail between Dolores and Ridgway. The San Juan National Forest Ranger station and a small city park are near the east end of town.

County Road #31 branches off Hwy. #145 within the Dolores city limits, providing access to McPhee Reservoir and the House Creek Campground and Recreation Area, 15 miles north. There is RV and tent camping, water, sanitary dump, boat ramp, and lots of good fishing and swimming. Beyond here, the Dolores-Norwood Road (F.R. #526) leads on to Groundhog Reservoir, connecting with other roads and trails heading farther north towards Lone Cone.

10.8

You are about to cross the Dolores River at the upper end of McPhee Reservoir. The dam was completed in 1984, creating the second largest body of water in Colorado. The 4,470 acre reservoir with its timbered shoreline, deep water, and numerous side canyons, provides excellent boating, fishing, skiing, swimming, and camping. To find out more about McPhee Reservoir, call 970-882-7296

The Dolores River Archaeological Project was conducted in an effort to rescue as much archaeological material as possible of the ancient Puebloan people that lived here before the flooding of the Dolores River Valley. This was the largest archaeological project ever conducted in this country, and the second largest in the world after the Aswan High project in Egypt before the flooding of portions of the Nile.

Most of the artifacts recovered here are housed in the Anasazi Heritage Center, located three miles north of Dolores on Hwy. #184.

From here you have two options for returning to Durango

Official route of the Skyway

9.2

From here the official route of the Skyway, Hwy. #145, continues on to Cortez where it intersects Hwy. #160 and heads east to Durango. Turn to the chapter titled *Dolores to Cortez to Durango--Official Route* to continue with the official route from Cortez to Durango.

Alternate Route
Hwy. #184 to Mancos

The alternate and somewhat shorter route follows Hwy. #184 from here south to Mancos where it intersects Hwy. #160 and heads east towards Durango. **This route bypasses Cortez and the entrance to Mesa Verde National Park.**

10.7

Here you are overlooking Cortez to the southwest. Straight ahead are the thousand foot cliffs of the Mesa Verde. To the west of the Mesa Verde is the pyramid-shaped Sleeping Ute Mountain, which is sacred to the Ute Indians, and beyond in the distance are the Chuska and Lukachukai Mountains on the boundary between Arizona and New Mexico. See m.m. # 8.4 in the chapter titled *Dolores to Cortez to Durango--Official Route* for a more in-depth description of the view from here.

12.2

Forest Service Road #556 is an improved road which heads northeast towards Haycamp Mesa, then loops east and south, connecting with F.R. #561, which you can follow past Transfer Campground and Jackson Gulch Reservoir to its connection with Hwy. #184 just north of Mancos.

17.6
At the Summit Reservoir State Wildlife and Fishing Area there are primitive campsites and a restroom, but no other facilities.

19.0
Hesperus Peak, the highest peak in the La Plata Mountains at 13,225 ft., dominates the skyline to the east. This is one of the four sacred directional peaks of the Navajo and is considered by them as their "Place of Emergence" from the previous world into this world.

23.9
The Millwood Road (C.R. #40) heads north about two miles, connecting with F.R. #559 upon entering the national forest. It then heads northeast, connecting with other forest service roads on the west side of the La Platas.

24.7
The Chicken Creek Road (C.R. #41) follows much the same route as C.R. #40 above. As with other roads that enter the national forest, there are numerous primitive campsites and hiking possibilities.

26.0
County Road # 42, which connects with FR. #561 at the national forest boundary, leads five miles to the Mancos State Recreation Area and Jackson Reservoir, with excellent boating, fishing,

and hiking. No swimming or skiing is allowed. Camping for RV's and tents is available. There are toilets and water but no electrical hookups. The Transfer N.F.S. Campground (l3 sites) is a few miles farther on F.R. #561.

The West Mancos Hiking Trail leaves the campground at the Transfer trailhead and drops immediately into the spectacular West Mancos River Canyon, which you can follow through a series of high cliffs for about two miles. Some of the largest specimens of quaking aspens in the world are right on the trail. Within a few miles this trail connects to other trails leading into the La Platas, as well as the Colorado Trail.

Want a unique experience? A few miles beyond Transfer Campground on F.R. #561 is the Jersey Jim Fire Lookout Tower, which served firewatchers from the 1940's through the 1970's. It has been renovated and furnished for overnight stays, and can be reserved by calling 970-533-7060.

At the intersection of Hwy 184 and Hwy 160 in Mancos you may turn right and proceed several miles to Mesa Verde National Park. After visiting the park you would return to Hwy 160 East to the original route.

Dolores to Cortez--Official Route

Following the Skyway (Hwy. #145) on to Cortez from m.m. #9.2 just west of Dolores:

8.1

Here Hwy. #184 leaves the Skyway and turns west towards the heart of Canyon Country around Monticello and Moab, Utah. The isolated mountains to the northwest are the Abajos, or "Blue Mountains", at the southern edge of Canyonlands National Park.

If you follow Hwy. #184 a ways, the Big Bend fishing access road to McPhee Reservoir is within a mile, and the Old McPhee Road fishing access is about two more miles. In another mile is the McPhee Recreation Area and Marina.

The Anasazi Heritage Center is a little over a mile north of this intersection on Hwy # 184. On display are many of the artifacts recovered during the Dolores River Archaeological Project. If you are interested in the Ancient Puebloan culture of this area, the Heritage Center shouldn't be missed. There are life-size dioramas depicting Anasazi dwellings, hands-on displays especially interesting to children, a short movie depicting the life of the area's ancient inhabitants, and a hologram based on a skull showing what these people really looked like. From here a short paved footpath leads to the Dominguez and Escalante Ruins. Call 970-882-5600 for information. The view from here is spectacular. (See the following entry.)

8.4

Continuing on towards Cortez on Hwy. #145 there is a panoramic view over much of the Four-Comers. The long, level ridge to the south is the Mesa Verde, the "Green Tableland", named by the 1776 Dominguez-Escalante Expedition, and the pyramid-shaped mountain to its right is the sacred Sleeping Ute. In it is seen the image of the "Great Warrior God" lying on his back with his feathered headdress flowing north. His arms are folded across his chest and his toes are visible to the south. In the distance between these two landmarks are the Chuska Mountains, spanning the border between New Mexico and Arizona. The spectacular gorges of Canyon de Chelly lie at their western base within the boundaries of the Navajo Nation.

Southwest about 50 miles "as the crow flies" is the Four-Corners National Monument, the only place in the U.S. where four states, Colorado, Utah, Arizona & New Mexico, meet.

Monument Valley is less than a hundred miles southwest, and Lake Powell is about 50 miles beyond that. The La Plata Mountains west of Durango dominate the skyline to the east. At 13,225 ft., Hesperus Peak, the tallest peak in the range, is easily identified. Called Debe'ntsa by the Navajo, it is the northern of the four sacred directional peaks that marks the boundaries of their ancestral homeland. The others are Mount Taylor (Tso'dzil) to the south in New Mexico, Blanca Peak (Sis na jin) to the east in Colorado's Sangre de Christo Range, and to the west are the San Fransisco Peaks (Dook Oslid) in Arizona.

Around the time the Pueblo people were abandoning the Four-Corners area, nomadic people from the north were migrating into the region. These Athabascan people from British Columbia later split into two groups which are seen in today's Apache and Navajo people whose lands are south of here.

Another local Native American Tribe is the Utes. There are two divisions of the Ute Tribe in Colorado; the Ute Mountain Utes, who occupy the region south of Cortez, and the Southern Utes, south of Durango. Their existence was first recorded by the Spanish in 1626. Known as the "Blue Sky People" by other tribes, the Utes were the uncontested rulers of Colorado's mountain wilderness. Their domain began on the eastern plains and stretched west 450 miles into Utah. Their exact origin is unknown, but their language is related to the Aztecs of Mexico. Today the Ute Tribes are the largest landowners in Colorado.

4.0
The highway is dropping into the valley of Cortez. Eight hundred years ago, the landscape in all directions was cultivated Anasazi fields of corn, beans and squash. This area was then home to around 40,000 people, which is about twice today's population. The population density of the "Ancient Ones" was possible due to their intimate relationship to the land and their expertise with dryland farming. There are many major ruins in the area such as Lowry, Escalante, Hovenweep, the Ute Mountain Ute

Tribal Park, Sand Canyon Pueblo and Mesa Verde, as well as hundreds of smaller ones.

Cortez

0.0

Welcome to Cortez. Plotted in 1886, the town had its first houses, school, restaurant, and boarding house within a year. Due to the dry climate of this area, dry-land farming much like that practiced by the Anasazi has been the most successful. Anasazi (Pinto) beans are one of the primary crops, and Dove Creek, 40 miles north, is known as the "pinto bean capital of the world".

At an elevation of 6,200 ft., Cortez is the lowest point on the Skyway. South and west the land drops off into the high desert and canyon country of the Colorado Plateau which covers an area the size of Ohio. Formed from the multi-colored sediments of ancient seas, this is an arid land of high plateaus and mesas with elevations generally ranging from 6,000 to 8,000 ft., though some plateaus rise to as much as 11,000 feet. Through this high desert, mighty rivers have cut deep, narrow canyons, formed broad, sheer-walled valleys, and sculptured the land into some of the world's most unique landscapes. To the Navajo it is the "land of rainbow's end".

Due to its proximity to many major archaeological sites, Cortez is often referred to as the "archaeological center of the United States". The Cortez Center/ University of Colorado Museum is on Market Street, one half block north of Main Street (Hwy. #160) in downtown Cortez. There is a small museum, special lectures, and a slide show, making this an excellent place to expand your knowledge of the ancient and contemporary cultures of the Four-Corners. For information, call 970-565-4048. The Cortez Visitor Center is on Main Street by the City Park, where Native American dances are performed on summer evenings.

Native American Dances

The Crow Canyon Archaeological Center is reached by following Hwy. #491 north from the west end of town. In a little over a mile is a sign directing you to the Center. You can participate in day programs that include an introduction to Anasazi culture, a tour of the laboratory, and a working excavation. Summer programs allow you to work with a professional archaeologist and participate in actual excavations. For information call 800-422-8975.

Cortez towards Mancos and Durango

From Cortez, the Skyway continues east on Hwy. #160 towards Mancos and Durango

41.8

Totten Reservoir, a state wildlife area and fishing lake, is less than a mile off the highway on CR #29. There are no facilities and no overnight camping.

43.4

McElmo Creek flows south of Cortez, then turns east into Utah, joining the San Juan River at Aneth. County Road G, which branches from Hwy. #160 on the south side of Cortez, follows McElmo Creek west past Sleeping Ute Mountain and through beautiful McElmo Canyon. Across from Battle Rock, about 15 miles west, a well-marked hiking trail leads into Sand and East Rock Creek Canyons. This pleasant hike leads through forests of pinyon and juniper, past colorful and fascinating rock formations, and into deep canyons with spring-fed pools where you will find ruins of the "Ancient Ones".

45.0

The high ridge of the Mesa Verde to the southeast is "Point Lookout".

46.4

On the north side of the highway is a large rest area with shaded picnic tables, restrooms, water, and a telephone.

48.0

The mountains in the distance to the west are the Abajo (Blue) Mountains near Blanding, Utah.

Mesa Verde National Park

48.2

Ahead is the entrance to Mesa Verde National Park, established in 1906 and now a United Nations World Heritage Cultural Site.

Here over a thousand years ago in this rugged land of steep walled, flat top mesas, isolated mountain ranges, deep canyon and little water, one of the most famous of Americas ancient cultures arose-the Anasazi (Ancestral Puebloans) of the Mesa Verde.

They built magnificent structures such as Cliff Palace, Square Tower House, Balcony House, Spruce Tree House, and Sun Temple. Over 20 major sites located on the mesa tops and in huge alcoves in the canyon walls are open to visitors. The Anasazi were deeply religious, wonderful weavers, potters, and builders. Visit the park and become acquainted with the world of the "Ancient Ones". Facilities include a museum, gift shop, campground (450 sites), lodge, and restaurants. For information, tune your radio to 1610 AM, or call 970-529-4465.

51.8
Here you cross Mud Creek, which joins the Mancos River a couple of miles south of the highway.

Mancos

54.6
This exit leads into the Mancos business district.

55.2
South of the highway is the old Diamond Match Factory, which once turned aspens into the most recognized brand of matches in the U.S.

56.1
Welcome to Mancos and the beautiful Mancos Valley, which the Dominguez/Escalante expedition described as having "abundant grass, tall timber, free-flowing streams, and snow-capped mountains". Because of its potential for grazing and agriculture, this was one of the first areas occupied by settlers after the peace treaty with the Utes. Captain John Moss was one of the earliest arrivals in 1873 with a group of California prospectors. Soon afterwards, Mormon cattlemen and ranchers from southeast Utah settled here and established the town of Mancos, making it one of the oldest towns in southwest Colorado.

U.S Hwy #160: Mancos to Durango

56.3

North of the highway is the Mancos Ranger Station and the San Juan National Forest Service Office. The marshes south of the highway provide an idea of what some of this area once looked like. Today they are home to a wide variety of wildlife. Notice the large beaver lodge in the pond.

56.7

You are about to cross the Rio de los Mancos, "The River of the Cripple", known today as the Mancos River. The river was given its name by the Dominguez/ Escalante Expedition when one of its members fell from his horse into the river and injured his arm. Other Spaniards had been here long before Escalante, and the river had earlier been known as the Rio de San Lazaro. The Mancos heads southwest, joining the San Juan River in New Mexico near Four-Corners National Monument.

In 1874 the famous photographer of the west, William Henry Jackson, accompanying the Hayden expedition, followed the river south a ways, where he took the first photographs of Anasazi cliff dwellings.

It was snowing hard on December 18, 1888, when Richard Wetherill and his brother-in-law, Charlie Mason, headed down this river into the Mesa Verde. This large plateau, cut by magnificent canyons rising above the Montezuma and Mancos valleys, was unknown except to the Indians. They were searching for lost cattle. What they found were the ancient "Cities" of the Anasazi, which are today protected in Mesa Verde National Park.

56.9

This exit leads into the small town of Mancos, located in the beautiful Mancos Valley. Mancos retains much of the feel of the days when cattle drives passed through town and cowboys whooped it up in the local saloons.

58.5

Echo Basin Road (C.R. #44) heads north about three miles where it connects with FR #566, an improved road leading into Echo Basin, at the western base of the La Platas. There are many opportunities for primitive camping and for further excursions into the backcountry on intersecting 4WD roads.

59.0

You are now on the western slope of Mancos Hill. To the north is Lost Canyon and the rocky outcroppings along Haycamp Mesa. Heading east, you will soon see the Mesa Verde south of the highway and Sleeping Ute Mountain to its right.

61.7

The Madden Peak Road (FR #316) is improved for about six miles before turning into a 4WD road ending in a couple more miles west of Madden Peak. There are good views to the south and west as the road gains elevation.

63.0

Here is the Target Tree N.F.S. Campground (51 sites). Long ago, this area was used by the Utes to harvest sap and the inner bark of the ponderosa pines for use as a food supplement. The trees were also used for target practice with rifles and bows & arrows. A historical marker points out the scarred trees that can still be seen. A trail from campsite #37 leads a short distance to the bed of the old narrow gauge railroad.

64.2

You can follow C.R. #105 south for a pleasant drive along Cherry Creek and enjoy the pastoral setting. When you reach the La Plata River, turn east and in a couple of miles you will intersect Hwy. #140, which you can follow back north to Hesperus, intersecting Hwy. #160 eleven miles west of Durango. The La Platas west of Durango loom ahead.

La Plata Mountains west of Durango

66.5

This historic marker commemorates one of the most famous expeditions in the history of the southwest. In 1776 Fathers Francisco V. Dominguez and Silvestre Velez de Escalante left Santa Fe in hopes of discovering a route to the Spanish missions of California. The journey lasted five months and covered 2,000 miles through the incredibly rough country of today's Four Corners region. Although the journey was a failure due to the rough terrain and the onset of winter, the expedition greatly influenced future explorations of the area.

67.5

The Cherry Creek Road (F.R. #568) leaves the highway here and loops back west for about 5 miles, connecting with the Madden Peak Road about a mile from the highway. Just ahead the Cherry Creek Picnic Area has 15 shady picnic sites surrounded by wild rose, gamble oak, and giant cottonwood trees.

71.0

The tall metal posts along the highway enable the snowplow crews to find their way during winter storms.

71.6

The Hesperus Ski Area and snowboard park is small but fun. For information call 970-259-3711.

72.2

C.R. # 124 leads into beautiful La Plata Canyon. A few miles up the road is the historic town of Mayday, founded when a mining boom began in the canyon in 1878. Beyond Mayday F.R #571 heads on up the canyon, eventually turning into a 4WD road leading to the summit of Kennebec Pass at 11,850 feet. There are breathtaking views of the San Juans, and you can intersect the Colorado Trail and other hiking trails leading into the La Platas. The Kroeger NFS Campground (10 sites) is a couple of miles above Mayday, and there are many primitive campsites as well as other 4WD roads which branch from the main road before the pass. These lead into side valleys with more wonderful scenery and relics from the old mining days.

Waterfalls in La Plata Canyon

It was up this canyon that Spanish explorers led by Juan Maria Antonio Rivera wandered in 1765 in search of riches. Finding evidence of silver, they named the mountains the "Sierra de la Plata", the "Silver Mountains".

72.5

Originating high in the La Plata Mountains to the north, the La Plata River flows south, joining the San Juan near Farmington, then west to the Colorado River at Lake Powell, then south to the Sea of Cortez.

72.8

Just south on Hwy. # l40 is the village of Hesperus, settled in 1882 with the opening of the Hesperus Coal Mine by John A. Porter. The site was named by the Rio Grande Southern Railroad for Hesperus Mountain to the northwest. Hesperus is Latin for "Evening Star".

Five miles south is the site of old Fort Lewis, established in 1880. It remained an army garrison until 1891, when it was converted into an Indian school which operated until 1911. In that year it became a public high school, and in 1927 college level education courses were added. In 1956 Fort Lewis College was moved to its present location on a bluff above Durango. There's a story of a Ute chief riding up one day and asking the Commanding Officer to loan him a cannon. The commander refused, saying he might use the cannon on the soldiers. "Naw" replied the chief. "Squaws chase soldiers off with sticks. Want cannon kill damn cowpunchers".

74.0

From the top of Mancos Hill, you drop 1,500 feet in elevation before reaching Durango. Far to the east are more lofty peaks of the San Juan Mountains in the area of Wolf Creek Pass, east of Pagosa Springs. The rolling ridges south of Durango are known as hogbacks, and are part of the Durango anticline, referring to a series of folds in the earth's crust caused by pressure. In this rugged country are places like Florida Mesa, Shellhammer Ridge, Piedra Peak, the Mesa Mountains, and La Boca Canyon. The small lake in the foreground is private.

The slopes of the La Plata Mountains north of the highway are largely scrub-oak today. In the 1870's, the southern slopes of these mountains were blanketed by the largest continuous stand of western yellow pine ever known, along with great stands of spruce and fir. By the early part of the 19th century, more than one billion board feet of lumber had been logged in this area.

76.1

The ridges to the southeast are the "Pictured Cliffs".

79.7

Heading into Durango, "Twin Buttes" is just ahead.

Perrins Peak is out of sight to the north. The town of Perrins was once located beyond Twin Buttes, and a spur of the Boston Colorado Railroad went around them to link the town with Durango.

79.0

C.R. #207 follows Lightner Creek for five miles. The only access to public land is about a mile from the highway, where you will intersect C.R. #208 leading into Perrins Peak State Wildlife Area. The road follows Dry Fork for about three miles, ending at the national forest boundary. No camping, mountain biking, or ATV's are allowed. This is an easily accessible but not heavily used area and you can often enjoy the peacefulness of wandering along the creek below the lofty buttes in complete solitude. In winter no snowmobiles are allowed and this is a good area for cross-country skiing.

80.5

The highway parallels Lightner Creek which joins the Animas River just west of Durango.

83.1

Just ahead, the highway crosses the Animas River which you saw just north of Durango as you headed towards Silverton. Just south of here is where the 1776 Dominguez-Escalante expedition crossed the river on their way west in search of a route from Santa Fe to the Spanish missions in California. From here the river flows south to join the San Juan just across the border in New Mexico. The waters then flow west to join the Colorado at Lake Powell on the Utah/Arizona border, then south again towards the Sea of Cortez. Across the river is Durango, and the junction of Hwys. #160 & #550.

Animas River south of Durango

The depot for the Durango-Silverton Narrow Gauge Railroad is just east of the intersection. One of the few narrow gauge trains still in existence, the trip from Durango to Silverton is a thrilling and nostalgic experience.

For information, call 888-872-4607.

Take a left here for a block, then right at the stoplight, and in two more blocks you'll again be on Main Street in downtown Durango.

I hope you've enjoyed the trip!

**Durango & Silverton Narrow-Gauge Train
Station in Durango**

Appendix

Altitude Sickness

Some people, especially those from lower elevations who have not adjusted to the mountains environment, are affected by altitude sickness from lack of oxygen at altitudes from around 7,500 ft. and higher. The symptoms are headache, nausea, vomiting, and lack of coordination. The best treatment is to return to lower elevations as soon as possible.

Clothing Suggestions

Expect the weather in the mountains from Spring through Fall to be generally sunny and pleasant during the days, though rain showers are common and there is always a chance of light snow. The nights will be cool to cold, depending on the elevation. Be aware that even in the summers the temperatures can drop 50 degrees in less than an hour when the sun sinks below the mountains. And remember that at high elevations the sun can be more intense than at the beach.

Take whatever clothing you feel is appropriate for your plans, but if you intend to do any extended hiking the following clothes are suggested:

Light jacket or wind breaker
Light weight but sturdy hiking boots
Long pants
Long sleeved shirt
Broad brimmed hat or cap
Warmer cap such as stocking cap

Bandanna
Sunglasses
Sunscreen

You should also have plenty of water, matches in a waterproof container, and some high-energy snacks

Camping

There are hundreds of miles of backcountry roads and trails for hiking, mountain-biking, horse packing, and jeeping in the San Juans. This guide will introduce you to locations which are easily accessible with most passenger cars from the Skyway and usually not requiring 4XD or high clearance. You will be advised in these situations. You will be traveling through both the San Juan and the Uncompahgre National Forests, and the purchase of a N.F.S map for these areas is suggested for those interested in exploring further into the backcountry, or just to provide an overall view of where you are. Rental jeeps for exploring beyond the limits of this guide are usually available in towns along the Skyway. For more information concerning backcountry byways, camping, fishing, or other uses of the national forests, check at the local visitor's center, National Forest Service stations, sporting goods stores, etc., along the drive.

Locations of National Forest Service campgrounds, phone #d's are given in the text as well as in the appendix. Phone numbers and additional information is also provided in the appendix. Most campgrounds in the national forests are "fee" campgrounds where tables, fire pits, grills, restrooms, and drinking water are provided. Most have spaces suitable for larger RV's.

Although the majority of N.F.S campsites are on a first-come-first-served basis, reservations in several campgrounds can be made by calling 877-444-6777. Reservations can be made up to 120 days in advance for individual sites, and 360 days for group sites. Most N.F.S campgrounds open in mid-May and close by October 1st, though some are open until November. There is unlimited "primitive" camping throughout the national forests as long as the campsite is at least 300 ft. from designated trails. There is no charge and there are no facilities.

National Forest Campgrounds

Durango to Silverton:
--Haviland Lake—17 miles north of Durango at m.m. #41.7
--Purgatory—24 miles north of Durango at m.m. #489
--Sig Creek—25 miles north of Durango and 6 miles off Hwy. at m.m. # 49.5

Silverton to Ouray:
--South Mineral Creek—2 miles north of Silverton and 4 miles off Hwy. at m.m. #72.3
--Amphitheatre—on south side of Ouray at m.m. #92.2

Ridgway:
--Ridgway State Park—just north of Ridgway on Hwy. #550

Telluride to Dolores:

--Sunshine—5 miles south of Telluride at m.m. #67.5

--Matterhorn—9 miles south of Telluride at m.m. #63.5

--Cayton—7 miles north of Rico at m.m. #54.5

--Burro Bridge, West Dolores, Mavresso, and Emmerson—these 4 campgrounds are on the West Dolores Road, which can be accessed at m.m. #24.5, 12 miles northeast of Dolores, and at m.m. #55.0, 7.5 miles north of Rico.

Mancos to Durango:

--Transfer—located off of Hwy. #184 north of Mancos at m.m. #26.1

--Target Tree—20 miles west of Durango at m.m. #63

--Kroeger—11 miles west of Durango at m.m. #72.2 then a few miles up

La Plata Canyon.

Several campgrounds are locate along the canyon road.

Useful Telephone #'s

Durango--Silverton Narrow Gauge
Train---888-872-4607
National Forest Campsite
Reservations------800-280-2267
Mesa Verde National Park-----970-529-4465

Police Departments
Durango ---970-375-4700
Silverton---503-873-5326
Ouray-------970-325-7272
Telluride---970-564-0548
Cortez------970-564-4044

State Highway Patrol
State-----------------970-385-1675
Durango-------------970-385-1675

For over 30 years Branson Reynolds has studied and explored throughout the west. His work has appeared in galleries, books, and publications such as Outside, Backpacker, the New York and LA Times, Time/Life books and on the Outdoor Channel. More information can be found about the trips he leads on his website at www.BransonReynolds.com.

You are welcome to contact Branson at
970-247-5274 or
www.Branson@BransonReynolds.com

No one knows the extravagantly beautiful San Juan Skyway country of southwest Colorado better than Branson Reynolds, and One Drive in a Million reflects that familiarity and affection in every page. Meticulously researched, written with mile-marker precision and beautifully photographed, One Drive in a Million is one guidebook in a million.

David Petersen
Author of Ghost Grizzlies and Living on the Wild Side of Nature

The San Juan Skyway

CPSIA information can be obtained
at www.ICGtesting.com
Printed in the USA
LVHW081935170821
695131LV00027B/218